May 2001

Dear Sally,

You continue to show what it means to be loving and nurturing ... through the years and through many seasons. You are also an example of how God has nurtured and cared for you and helped you grow. This little book commemorates that and. I hope can be useful to bring you joy from your garden.

Thank you for being a wonderful mother and mother-in-law!

Much love,
Rita

THE
FLOWERING
YEAR

ANNA PAVORD

THE FLOWERING YEAR

A Guide to Seasonal Planting

CROSS RIVER PRESS
A Division of Abbeville Press, Inc.
NEW YORK

First published in the United States of America by
Cross River Press, a division of Abbeville Press, Inc.,
488 Madison Avenue, New York, N.Y. 10022.

First published in the United Kingdom by Chatto & Windus,
20 Vauxhall Bridge Road, London, England.

ISBN 1-55859-240-7

CONTENTS

ACKNOWLEDGEMENTS

THE IDEA FOR THIS BOOK AROSE FROM A SERIES OF ARTICLES on monthly planting schemes which I wrote originally for the *Independent*. I am most grateful to the editor for allowing me to develop material that first appeared in the paper.

The influences that shape one's ideas are not always clear, but I am unequivocally aware of a great debt to gardeners such as Christopher Lloyd and Graham Stuart Thomas whose writing makes one look at even the most familiar plants with fresh eyes.

My thanks are due to Rupert Lancaster, Amanda Horton and the editorial team at Chatto for their support and encouragement, and to Sara Robin, the designer. Penny David smoothed out the hiccups in the text and Tony Lord, king of nomenclature, undertook the arduous task of checking and updating all the plant names.

Finally I must thank my daughters, Oenone, Vanessa and Tilly. They all have a good line in bad jokes. I hope none of them remain in the text.

To my husband Trevor Ware

INTRODUCTION

THE WAY THAT PLANTS ARRIVE IN THE GARDEN IS NOT ALWAYS A well ordered affair. Some plants have squatters' rights, established long before we, the new garden owners, arrived upon the scene. Others arrive as presents and have to be found a home to avoid difficulties and injured silences later in the season. A Sunday visit to another garden, a random trip to a local nursery provides an irresistible opportunity to buy plants. It is hardly surprising that this is a more satisfying exercise than spending money on plastic bin liners. And it is extremely pleasant to wander round the garden in the aimless way that maddens non-gardeners, with memories ricocheting from plant to plant. Here is the viburnum that the dog was sick on in the car, there the Christmas present azalea, there a stand of *Verbena bonariensis*, raised precariously from seed on the kitchen windowsill.

Unfortunately, randomness brings its own difficulties. You may well find yourself with a garden in which there is nothing happening from August to May. It is tempting, in the great surge that pushes us irresistibly towards garden centres at Easter time, to pick up only those plants that are already in flower. This is not a sound policy. You will get an astounding show for a month after Easter, certainly, but what then ? You will not be giving the plants themselves the best chance in life either, if you plant them in flower. While it is fully occupied in keeping a display going above ground, a plant has little energy left to sort itself out below ground. It is better to let plants settle in their new homes, put out some feeders and anchors around them before they are called on to perform. In the long term, you will get stronger plants and better displays of flowers in subsequent seasons.

The received wisdom is clear. Bearing in mind the site, the soil, the different aspects of the garden, the presence or absence of wind and frost, the gardener should draw up a list of suitable trees, shrubs and herbaceous plants. The problem, particularly for new gardeners, is in knowing what to put on the list. Again, sources of inspiration may be random: the next-door neighbour's garden, an illustration in a magazine. Even those whose horticultural knowledge does not extend beyond recognizing a daffodil will bring to their plots a Proustian jumble of *plantes perdues*: the memory of a particular smell, acid American currant or sweet summer jasmine, the image of a particular silhouette, magnolia in blossom against a suburban sky. From all these sources and from books and magazine articles, you may begin to make your lists. After a while, you may even buy a special notebook for the purpose, marked from A–Z, and transcribe into it all the jottings you made on the back of your chequebook and the yellowing scraps of paper torn from magazines in the dentist's waiting room. But what do you do then ? You may begin to buy plants, starting methodically at the beginning of the notebook, but the consequences of this are clear. You will have in the garden so many plants beginning with A – abelia, abutilon, anemone, aquilegia – that you will never get round to the delights of L (lavender, lily) let alone T (tellima, tulip).

Unless you are specifically a collector, it is easier to plant a garden by concentrating on a specific patch of ground rather than by working entirely from lists. Even if you are careful enough to order from your list a variety of plants that together will give you pleasure through twelve months of the year, your plantings will have much more impact, have a stronger, more dramatic effect, if you group plants of a particular season together, rather than dotting them around the garden at random, marooned as single, struggling artistes in a sea of non-performers. Think of the garden as a stage set, with the spotlight shifting from one area to the next as the months move on. On the March set, dressed in yellow and green, are corylopsis, hellebores and euphorbia, with an underplanting of blue *Anemone blanda*. As April comes, the spotlight shifts and moves to another part of the garden where japonica is waiting to take over the lead, with a supporting cast of daffodils, tulips and creeping epimedium. There will be sideshows going on, too; a scattering of aubrietia perhaps in a different part of the garden, unlinked to the main March event. As April's early tulips die away, you may plan to revitalize the spot later on with a snatched display of annuals, shaggy asters perhaps, but the asters, on the old April set, will be an extra in September, when the main spotlight will be concentrated on a different part of the garden. You may want eventually to drape a late-flowering clematis over one of the shrubs used for your April or May schemes, to give the patch an extra lift after its chief season has passed and to provide a diversion from the main August show which will be happening elsewhere. Late-flowering clematis are useful in this role as old untidy growths can be cut hard back in February so that they do not get in the host shrub's way when it comes on for its own, earlier star turn.

The rest of the garden, of course, does not disappear, even if the focus of attention is drawn to one particular spot. You have to make sure that each seasonal group contains some plant that contributes for a longer spell than its brief flowering season. This is an excellent discipline. It makes you think about and look at plants in an entirely different way. Flowers are a seducing but evanescent part of a tree or shrub's personality. A plant's shape, habit of growth, foliage and possible fruit should all be taken into account when you are awarding points. Annuals we judge rather differently. Here, flower power is all, but even in this group there are sometimes other assets. Nigella, or love-in-a-mist, has very pretty filigree foliage and splendid seed-heads, both of which are only slightly less important than the sky-blue flowers. Both stretch the plant's season of usefulness far beyond the season of flowering. Where shrubs are concerned, foliage becomes even more important. You need to think about evergreen leaves and what they might do for the garden. Too much in a small space would be overpowering, too little gives the garden a curiously unfurnished, impermanent air. The foliage of herbaceous plants also has an important part to play. You may include hemerocallis, the day-lily, in a July planting scheme, because of its showy trumpet flowers in yellow, orange and red; already in February, however, the lush, pale green spears of its leaves will be pushing through the ground. At this early season they are a pleasure in themselves after months of bare ground. So, by grouping plants for seasonal effect, you must not abandon all thought of what the garden as a whole will be looking like. You will quickly recognize your allies in this task. *Euphorbia characias wulfenii* may well be the star of your April or May act with its huge heads of sulphurous flowers. But the plant has such style, holds itself so well and, constantly renewing itself with fresh growth from the base, such staying power, it will remain a tower of strength throughout the year. *Choisya ternata*, the Mexican orange blossom, might also be brought in as a May star, because of its heads of white, sweetly scented flowers which bloom at that season. The excellent foliage, glossy, evergreen, held in three-fingered hands, and the pleasing overall shape of the shrub, balanced and rounded, will ensure that the May set will not look abandoned even when the spotlight has moved on to an August happening. At a much lower level is the little autumn-flowering cyclamen, *C. hederifolium*. In this book it is included in a September group with caryopteris and abelia. September is the season for its swept-back flowers, miniature versions of the well-known florist's cyclamen, but equally important in the garden are the splendid marbled leaves, ivy-shaped, that spring up as the flowers are finishing and furnish the ground for another six months at least. As on the stage, the rest of the cast do not disappear when the star says his lines. They are still there though not at that moment playing a major role.

It is important to distinguish between garden design and planting. This is not a book about garden design. It will tell you nothing about mass and void, or about constructing lines of sight. Its sole concern is with ways of using plants to create a whole series of seasonal effects. The effects will be immeasurably enhanced if you first give proper attention to the space in which the plants will be displayed and the way that this space is divided up. Faced with a plot of ground to turn into a garden, a new gardener's instinct is to tackle the edges first, to work round the boundary, planting as he goes. It may be the remnant of some atavistic urge to mark territory: dogs lift legs; we plant clematis. Whatever the reason, it often leads to a particular kind of layout: borders, usually too narrow to build up any depth in plant groups, all the way round the edge of the plot and a path making another circuit round the inside edge of the border. Whatever ground is left becomes the lawn. The centre of this garden thus becomes a centre by default, not so much a designed shape as a random happening. If you think from the centre of the space out towards the boundaries, quite different patterns may emerge. You may start with the thought of a rectangular paved area in the middle of the plot with more flower borders on either side reaching to the boundaries. You may see a path up through the centre of the garden, the length divided by upright screens of trellis either side of the path, so that the width of the garden spreads and narrows as you pass down the path between the trellis screens and into the spaces contained beyond them. There could perhaps be raised beds round the three-sided shapes made by trellis screens and boundary wall, with different bays peaking in terms of display at different times of the year.

These are simple ways of manipulating the standard rectangular shape of the majority of back gardens, using the same basic ingredients of paths, flower beds and grass that crop up in outside-in gardens. But by thinking of the centre first, you may end up with an arrangement that gives you more opportunities for imaginative planting and, consequently, more pleasure. Novice gardeners are usually told that they must draw out a plan on paper before they start flailing around with spades and wheelbarrow. Because this is the way that professional garden designers work, it has been assumed that this is also the best way forward for amateurs. Not necessarily. Paper designs get over-complicated. Interlocking circles ooze out over the page. A bare space becomes a threat to creativity. The obvious is avoided at all costs. 'Features', as designers call them, start bobbing up all over the place. To achieve its full effect, a feature should be used as sparingly as an ultimatum.

Another difficulty with paper is that it cannot contain the information you need to make the right decisions and which you get as you prowl your patch. You take in the slight rises and falls in the ground and the consequences that these will have on your design. You are aware of things beyond your boundary that you would rather not see and can work out more easily how these might be disguised with particular plants. Above all, working on the ground, it is easier to develop a sense of proportion and understand the importance of a space where nothing is happening. A planned void is very different to a void by default and nothing may be just the thing to set off some plants, such as the splendid cardoon, which are best seen in isolation, like sculptures. Professional designers would never get clients to pay for a couple of days walking about rubbing their noses. Time is the advantage that amateurs have and when it has been well spent, mulling over possibilities and adaptations, sticks and string and hosepipe on the ground may prove better design tools than pencil and paper. When the garden has been arranged into a series of satisfying interlocking shapes, then you can begin to colour them in.

The size of each month's plant group will depend entirely on the scale of the garden into which it is put. The suggestions that follow in the succeeding chapters are starting points only. You can add or subtract as necessary. In a tiny garden, one *Magnolia stellata* underplanted with a carpet of pale blue scillas may be all there is room for in March. If the garden theatre is a large one, the garden director might want to create an altogether more extravagant production, adding a tree behind the magnolia, a clump of *Euphorbia amygdaloides robbiae*, a small stand of leucojum. Certain accommodating plants such as ferns and violas that have a long season of interest are useful for swelling plant groups. March is too early for them, but either could be included in the plant groups suggested from May to September. In a large garden too, there will be more opportunity to experiment with special effects for autumn and winter, planting trees with ornamental bark and evergreens such as hollies for their brilliant winter livery of dark glossy green and red. In a small garden, the greatest effort will usually be concentrated on the months when the garden is most in use, though the rest of the year must not be entirely forgotten.

Once, in the largest gardens, whole areas were set aside for one type of plant – the iris garden, the Michaelmas daisy garden – opened up while they were at their peak and then shut off, unvisited by the family until the appropriate season came round again. William Robinson, author of *The English Flower Garden* (first published in 1883) and scourge of those who liked their gardens neatly bedded out and strictly controlled, laid out his garden at Gravetye Manor in just this way. The spring display was centred on the four-acre meadow garden to the south of the house. Then the rhododendrons in the east garden bordering the drive took over, followed by the azaleas in an entirely different part of the garden, the bank to the north of the formal garden. By high summer the spotlight had moved to the richly planted flower beds in the formal garden to the west of the manor house and the garden's year ended with the autumn colour of trees in the heath garden. At Chatsworth, where lack of space is not a problem to keep the Duchess of Devonshire awake at night, there is a wonderfully riotous lupin garden, peaking in June and July.

Although most of us garden in spaces very much smaller than Chatsworth or Robinson's thirty acres at Gravetye, the same principle can still be brought to bear in a small garden. Even in a tiny space, it is better to have plants grouped to make the maximum effect at their particular season. In July, instead of having a phlox flowering in one corner, a day-lily in another and an alchemilla in a third spot, bring them all together, so that each enhances the other. The impact of the total will be far greater than any of the separate parts. Even if you garden entirely in pots and windowboxes, the same principle applies. Your winter effect may be a single camellia, brought to the fore in its tub when its buds and flowers are at their most spectacular. When the flowers finish, the tub can be moved into a less prominent position where the camellia's foliage can provide a glossy background for other tubs moved in their turn into the limelight. In May you could adapt one of the planting schemes detailed in a later chapter and fill a tub with fat double daisies interplanted with pale blue puschkinias, or forget-me-nots mixed with a pale yellow viola such as 'Moonlight'. In July a tub of splendid lilies would be, on their own, enough to carry the star's mantle. The violas from May might still be flowering but May's pot will now have been shunted into the sidelines. In autumn, a Japanese maple, perhaps the startling 'Senkaki' planted in ericaceous compost in an oriental glazed pot, will provide a blaze of colour, but will also have given a useful service since spring, making a soft foliage background to the lilies perhaps, or some other jazzy star.

Planting a garden is a three-dimensional business and it may help to think of each group as a three-tiered cake, with plants growing at three different levels. Trees and shrubs will make up the tallest and possibly the most wide-spreading top tier. Smaller shrubs and herbaceous perennials fill in on the middle ground, while small bulbs and ground-cover plants provide the third and lowest layers of planting. On each monthly showing, there may be room for only one shrub and perhaps three perennials, but in the same space on the ground you could fit in four different groups of bulbs or ground-cover plants. A patch 6 x 4ft/1.8 x 1.2m, well fed and well watered, could in this way support eight different plants. Half-standard trees, with trunks that rise clear out of the ground for 4–5ft/1.2–1.5m before they begin to branch, are much easier to plant under than low-branched trees. Trees with light, airy canopies, such as amelanchier, steal little light or sun from plants growing underneath their branches. Whitebeams are far more dense. These are considerations that need to be faced when building up plant groups. Bulbs have little part to play in the garden when their flowers are over. Fortunately they realize this and obligingly dive underground for at least half the year. Where bulbs are used in the bottom tier of planting, they will need companion plants, epimediums perhaps if the conditions are right, to furnish the ground in their absence.

Again, the size of the garden will be the most important limiting factor on the way that you work. Trees and shrubs are less easy to accommodate than bulbs, but for the most satisfying effects, you need plants working at all three levels. It would be a pity in a small garden to abandon shrubs altogether for the sake of cramming more plants in on the ground storey: the final effect would be too busy. The larger bulwarks of hydrangea, chaenomeles, viburnum or whatever they might be, are needed as calm, fixed points, to take the garden up into the third dimension of volume, which little scillas and violas scrabbling around, however endearingly, on the ground floor cannot do. Because of their overall form, some shrubs are easier to use than others. Choisya is a brilliant shrub, but because it grows in a bun shape, furnishing itself down to the ground with evergreen foliage, you cannot plant underneath it: it occupies the whole of the ground it sits on. A viburnum such as 'Lanarth' or 'Mariesii' is ideally suited for three-tiered planting. It holds its branches in a stiffly horizontal way, at right angles to the main stem, so that when it flowers in May and June there is plenty of room under them to tuck other plants – omphalodes or violas or variegated ground-hugging lamium – close to its main stem under the spreading branches. It may have the same girth as the choisya, but is more economical to use, because that girth is not sitting on the ground.

You need to think about each plant's habit when you are building up seasonal plant groups. No specific positions have been worked out or ground plans prepared in the following chapters. Instead you will get two or three suggestions for plant associations in each monthly section, using trees, shrubs, flowers, bulbs and ground cover, all of which will be at their peak around that time, though some will continue to contribute for a longer season. Specific ground plans can only be fitted into specific places in the garden, but the intention of this book is to suggest plant groups that, if you take the trouble to understand what the plants themselves need, can be adapted for several different situations. In a patch of border backed by a fence, for instance, you will naturally not want to lose all your small, bottom-tier plants at the back of the border, entirely blocked out by the bulk of a shrub at the front. The shrub might be best in the middle of the patch, the tree behind and slightly to one side of it, with some of the bottom-tier plants wandering to the back of the border, but most of them to the front, where they can be properly admired. All groups of plants need to be built up bearing in mind how you will be looking at that piece of ground. If you are making up groups in an island bed, you will arrange your plants differently, as you will be seeing them from all angles of a 360-degree circle. When you view a border made against a boundary, you can only see it from half that number of angles. In an island border, there is no 'back' so the tree might occupy the centre, with middle-tier plants mostly round the outer edge.

The 'mostly' is an important reservation. You do not want groups to be arranged too mechanically, with an inevitable grading of height from the centre down to the edges. If a middle-tier plant has particularly good form or texture, or some other quality that you like, bring it forward and let it take a front seat. If the weather is suitable and the ground pleasantly damp, there is no reason why you should not reshuffle the elements of the group if you want, whatever the time of year. If you take up enough earth with the roots and pay attention to watering afterwards, plants are remarkably forgiving of these changes of direction. It is often at the very season of flowering, rather than at the planting time in spring, that you realize how you could better have arranged things.

Some indication is given in the text where plant groups are suitable for shade. Shade is not a problem – the lack of it is more so – provided you choose the right plants to put in it. The most important thing is to ask yourself constantly, 'What does this plant need in order to flourish?' Some plants have quite specific needs (the huge family of rhododendrons, for instance, which demand acid soil); others are happy-go-lucky and thrive in all soils and all situations. In making up groups of plants, you cannot think merely in designer terms of pools of yellow making a contrapuntal statement against a wall of blue, both of them shining out of a dark corner, backed by evergreens. Your pool of yellow is not inert fabric or paint, but a collection of living creatures, which can thrive or die, depending, in part, on how well their needs are met. To a great extent, that is the gardener's responsibility. Aconites may well make your pool of yellow in a dark corner. Crocus may not. One is happier in shade than the other. Often some knowledge of a plant's natural habitat gives important clues to the ways in which it can be used in the garden.

Because plants are living things, extremely responsive to factors such as rain or the lack of it, sun, frost, air temperature, flowering times may fluctuate from one year to the next. Geography also dictates performance. Even in a relatively small country such as

Britain there is often a three-week difference in flowering times between the north and the south of the country. In this book, plants have been allotted particular months. Chaenomeles appears as one of the ingredients in an April planting. Roses find a place in June. Yet there are extraordinary seasons when both might be flowering in December, the rose extending its season onwards, the chaenomeles leaping into action several months earlier than usual. The spring season is particularly difficult to pin down, as a mild winter or a series of harsh frosts can advance or retard flowering considerably. A summer of drought will sometimes telescope July and August plants into June, as the flowers, sensing trouble, struggle to set seed before they are stopped in their tracks by thirst. This may cause slight hiccups in the smooth production of successive acts on your garden stage. The gardener should not feel cheated when plants do not perform to cue. Their ideas are often rather better than our own.

MARCH

ALL GARDENERS SUFFER FROM THE DELUSION THAT THE GARDENING open season starts in March. Unless you have the constitution of a polar bear, you will have to fuel the delusion by sleight of hand with seed packets indoors. Outside, despite the example set by the big crocuses that unbutton with abandon at the slightest glimpse of the sun, it is usually too cold for the sort of ruminative rambling that is what gardeners most enjoy about their gardens. No other month fluctuates so wildly between the depths and heights of weather as March. You know that nothing good can be expected of November, but it is all too easy to be persuaded on a balmy March day that spring has arrived. Plants are taken in too. They are triggered into growth when the average daily temperature rises above 43°F/8°C. There have been plenty of years when fresh leaves of hydrangea and clematis and roses have cheerfully believed March's promise to show them a good time and then been dumped rather suddenly by a prolonged bout of north-westerly gales or a succession of freezing snowstorms. Only in the lowlands of Cornwall can March truly be said to bring spring. The rest of us still feel winter's cold seeping inexorably through the soles of our boots as we stop to admire a camellia, a crocus, a clutch of polyanthus or any other of March's offerings.

March's coming often sets off a flurry of horticultural resolutions. Some, such as the determination to clean all gardening tools before putting them away for the day, are too impossibly virtuous ever to have a chance of succeeding. Other more pragmatic resolutions are not so demanding: to dead-head the roses regularly, to mulch the clematis, to experiment with more annuals grown from seed, to start a gallery of topiary figures. One of the most important resolutions we can make is to consider a plant's needs before our own. This may stop us from murdering some perfectly willing plants by putting them in the wrong place. The first great lesson for new gardeners to learn when choosing plants for seasonal displays is the one about acid-loving plants. This is particularly pertinent in this early part of the year, when camellias are shamelessly and irresistibly flaunting their delights in nurseries and garden centres. Camellias can be a star turn in March, but before you succumb completely, ask yourself a few questions. First of all – soil. Have you got what it takes to produce a healthy plant with shiny dark green foliage and plenty of flowers? Camellias, like the pieris and rhododendrons that follow hard on their heels, like an acid soil with a pH between 5 and 6.5. (The letters stand for potential of hydrogen and they measure the relative acidity and alkalinity of soil on a scale stretching from 1 to 14.) The second big question is where to plant. In the wild, camellias grow under the protection of a high forest canopy and the principle of sheltered shade should not be jettisoned if you want to use them as the centrepiece of a March display. They will withstand an occasional gale, but hate continuous draughts. The soil should remain moist, but drainage must be irreproachable. There should be plenty of humus available. Leaf mould is ideal, peat second best. A north-facing wall, perhaps in a sheltered courtyard, may be just the place. Avoid a position such as an east-facing wall where early sun may catch frost-bound blooms. These caveats make it seem a prima donna among plants: it is not. A camellia is like a computer. If you create exactly the right programme for it, it will whirr away with no problems. If there is a tiny maladjustment in the schedule, it goes to pieces.

Some power-crazed gardeners, with ground that is basically alkaline, try to persuade camellias to feel at home by excavating pits and filling them with special ericaceous compost before planting. Unfortunately, after a time, even with regular doses of a tonic such as sequestrene, the chemical substances in the ordinary soil leach into the prepared pit and the camellia begins to mope, the foliage becoming blotched and yellow. It is a sad sight. Gardeners with alkaline soils determined to grow camellias for their March display would do better to keep them in tubs filled with special compost and trundle them on at the appropriate time for their party piece.

The next hurdle is to choose a variety that is more likely to thrive than not. Of the several thousand types available, more than half will be too tender to grow successfully outside in the UK. A different half will have such violent forms or colours that you would not want them anyway. There is an increasing tendency among breeders to go for flower size above all other considerations, such as proportion and form. This has introduced a coarseness which nature never intended. Varieties of *Camellia x williamsii* and *C. japonica* are best for using in the garden. Out of the favoured south-west of the country, the more tender *C. sasanqua* and *C. reticulata* types are better under glass. Flowers are roughly classified into different types: single, semi-double, anemone-form, full peony form and so on. The more complicated sorts are unlikely to weather well outside. Whites are touchier than reds about frost, wind and wet. In the north, choose tough *C. x williamsii* varieties such as 'Leonard Messel' (deep pink loose peony form), 'J. C. Williams' (single pale pink), 'Brigadoon' (semi-double deep pink), the faithful 'Donation' (semi-double soft pink), Donation's daughter 'Rose Parade' (deep rose peony form), or 'St Ewe' (bright rose pink single). 'Donation' is the most popular camellia in Britain, in flower from late February through until May. It is an upright and rather sparse plant, but very free-flowering.

A camellia stops growing at about the end of July. It then settles to the business of producing flower buds for the following spring – or not, as the case may be. This is a cause of frustration to camellia owners. Dryness at the roots will certainly inhibit the process, and it is vital to keep camellias well watered between July and September. Too liberal a hand with nitrogen feed may also interfere with flower bud production. Some varieties such as 'Bow Bells' and 'Charity' are notably more free-flowering than others. *C. x williamsii* types are the most reliable, though some, such as 'Elsie Jury' and 'Fragrant Pink', need plenty of sun to set and ripen flower buds. Varieties of *C. japonica* may be shy flowering when young, but give a good display after four or five years.

It is a measure of the plant's great beauty, when happy, that we do so much to get it to perform well. The battle has been going on for a long time. The first camellia flowered in England in 1739, for Lord Petre at Thorndon Hall in Essex. It must have died shortly thereafter, because the camellia got no more publicity until the beginning of the nineteenth century, when Alfred Chandler did a great deal of hybridizing at his nursery at Vauxhall. He had one of the biggest collections of camellias in the country. The mistake the Victorians made was to suppose that all camellias needed cover and heat. Special houses were built for them and, under glass, the new species brought in by Robert Fortune and others were quietly cooked to death. Camellias will grow perfectly well in an unheated conservatory, and, if you have such a thing, and are short of space for planting outside, this may be the way to ensure your March display, with camellias blooming unblemished under cover, where you can hover and admire and titivate them without your fingers dropping off with cold. Always use rainwater for conservatory camellias: the calcium in tap water upsets their programme. Plants in pots can be moved outside between May and October. If camellias are planted in permanent quarters in a conservatory, allow them to rest for about six weeks after flowering, without food or too much water.

Feed plants in tubs with weak liquid fertilizer every two weeks from the time they finish flowering until the end of August. Where plants are growing in open ground, scatter dried blood round the roots in April, when the soil is damp, and mulch with pine needles, leaf-mould or dead camellia flowers. Some swear by tea leaves, for tea is a member of the same family. If you have got the preliminaries right, after-care will be minimal. No regular pruning is needed, though you can snip off any lopsided shoots in April. Aphids and scale insects may cause sooty mould, which forms on the leaves under the places where the dread pests are quartered. Malathion will see off the bugs, but you may need to wash the leaves to get rid of the mould, rubbing them gently with your thumbs. Propagate by cuttings of half-ripe wood from June to August. Branches may also be layered in September.

Used outside, camellias do not need distracting companions. A scattering of plants at ground level, those that have no pretensions to be stars themselves, will be sufficient. The advantage of using one of the *C. x williamsii* family as your centrepiece is that flowers, sensibly, drop off as they die. Most camellias hang grimly on to their dead blooms and, unless you snip them away as they fade, end up looking hideously funereal. If you choose the deep pink 'Leonard Messel', use clumps of a gentle bulb underneath, nothing too distracting, perhaps an early form of Star of Bethlehem, *Ornithogalum balansae.*

Mainly yellow and blue

For an entirely different scheme in yellow, green and blue, choose for the top tier lemon-yellow *Forsythia suspensa*, or, if you feel that any forsythia is too bilious, *Corylopsis pauciflora* with soft drooping bunches of very pale flowers. Fill in the middle with *Helleborus argutifolius* and leathery dark-leaved *Euphorbia amygdaloides robbiae*. Underplant at ground level with blue *Anemone blanda* or large fat purple crocus. Yellow and blue is a satisfying combination in the garden and there is plenty of opportunity in March to dabble with mixes : Roman hyacinths, early daffodils, scillas, knitted together with the sharp, acid-green tones of the euphorbia flower heads. If forsythia were more difficult to grow, gardeners would croon over it. Instead it blooms as wholeheartedly on railway embankments and on forgotten dumps as it does in the most manicured front garden. Its cause is not helped by having, as it often does, the violent pink cherry 'Kanzan' as its neighbour. Forsythia with blue and green, rather than pink, is transformed. It does not have much to recommend it for the rest of the year, as the leaves are no more than leafish and the shrub not of any particular form. But, when in doubt, reach for clematis. This can be thrown at the forsythia to bloom in late summer and will be most grateful for a support to hang on to. In February, before the forsythia's moment of glory arrives, you will be able to cut down the clematis stems and free the shrub from the tangle of

1 *Forsythia*

DECIDUOUS SHRUB
HEIGHT AND SPREAD
8 x 8 FT/2.4 x 2.4 M
ZONE 6–9

The one shrub that everybody can recognize at a hundred paces, though not everyone loves it. 'Lynwood' is an extremely free-flowering variety with larger flowers than the ordinary type. *F. suspensa* has lax, arching branches, easily trained against a wall. Plant in autumn or spring, in sun or partial shade. Remove some

old wood after flowering in April and shorten the side growths of *F. suspensa*. Propagate by hardwood cuttings in October. *F. suspensa* often layers itself where the ends of branches touch the ground.

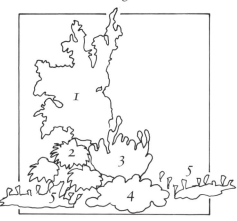

2 *Helleborus argutifolius* (syn. *H. corsicus*)

EVERGREEN PERENNIAL
HEIGHT AND SPREAD
24 x 24 IN/60 x 60 CM
ZONE 6–9

Fully hardy, handsome plant, tolerant of a wide range of growing conditions. Avoid, however, situations that are either very wet or very dry. A lime soil suits them slightly better than an acid one, and shade better than blazing sun. They hate disturbance. Mulch regularly in spring with leaf-mould or compost, rather than peat. Use bonemeal as a general fertilizer in autumn. Cut out old flowered stems in late spring, unless you want to collect seed, which is the best way of propagating plants. Sow it as soon as it is ripe. It may germinate in autumn, or may wait until the following year. Spray with fungicide if there are any signs of the black blotches of leaf spot.

3 Euphorbia amygdaloides robbiae (Mrs Robb's bonnet)

EVERGREEN PERENNIAL
HEIGHT AND SPREAD
18 X 24IN/45 X 60CM
ZONE 7–9

This spurge is an excellent colonizer, though it has a mind of its own. It thrives in a wide range of conditions including deep shade, but will appreciate a mulch of compost in spring. Cut out dead stems as necessary and propagate by digging up stems that have strayed away from their original site.

4 Anemone blanda

TUBER
HEIGHT AND SPREAD
6 X 10IN/15 X 25CM
ZONE 7–9

Delicately ethereal daisy flowers in white, pink or blue with deeply divided, grey-green foliage. They are happy in acid or alkaline soil, but are fussier about its texture. Soil should be neither too wet nor too dry. Leaf-mould or old compost worked into the soil before planting will help immeasurably. The tubers are usually available in autumn. If they seem very dry, soak them overnight before planting, setting them no more than

3–4cm deep. Once they are established, they are best left alone, apart from an annual top dressing of leafmould each autumn. 'Atroca-erulea' is a good deep violet-blue, very free-flowering, but as good as any of the named varieties are cheaper buys usually labelled more vaguely *A. blanda* blue.

5 Crocus

CORM
HEIGHT AND SPREAD
4 X 4IN/10 X 10CM
ZONE 4–9

Over-deep planting is one of the most common reasons why crocuses fail to flower. That and depredations by mice, who are monsters where crocus are concerned. Traps baited with chocolate, which they like even more than crocuses, are the simplest way to catch them: poison is altogether more sinister. Plant corms in the autumn as soon as they are available, setting them no more than 2in/5cm deep. Do not cut down leaves before they are dead, or pull off withering flowers. The big fat Dutch crocus will be too bossy to use with the anemones. If you want both, choose a more delicate species crocus such as *C. chrysanthus* or *C. tomasinianus* which will start to appear in February. The narrow furled buds of *C. tomasinianus* open flat out in the sun to show off their brilliant orange stigma. 'Barr's Purple' and 'Whitewell Purple' are deeper in colour.

growth. After having faced up squarely to its shortcomings, you can coast downhill on the list of its merits. It is one of the few shrubs that you can cut copiously to bring inside the house without feeling guilty. Whoever thinks of cutting a branch of camellia ? A flower may be snipped off here and there, but no more. Forsythia will leap into bloom inside from bare brown stems and this is a cheering characteristic. We should also be grateful, rather than despising it, for its easy-going nature. There are enough plants that have the sulks in a year's planting schemes to keep any gardener happy. Make the most of forsythia's obliging habit of growing in sun or partial shade and in a wide range of soils. *Forsythia suspensa* has lax, drooping stems and can easily be persuaded to scramble through dark holly or yew. Grown like this it may reach 20ft, draping its host with festoons of yellow in a most graceful way. Or it will grow against a wall, if this is what you have got. In this way, with the forsythia pinned flat against a support, there will be the maximum amount of room for foreground planting. The corylopsis can also be trained against a wall, preferably a south or west one, where it will have some protection from cold winds. It is not as easy-going as forsythia. If you have no suitable wall, grow it under the shelter of an overhanging tree or where more stalwart companions can shield it from draughts. It likes slightly acid soil. The little bunches of flowers smell of cowslips.

The statuesque hellebore *H. argutifolius* flowers in March and April, but is an asset all the year, for it makes a splendid, sculptural mass and has excellent foliage, three-lobed, thick and spiny. It is evergreen in the sense that when you cut away the old leaves with the spent flowering stems in late spring, the new foliage is already taking its place. The old name, *H. corsicus*, signifying where it lived (Corsica) has been replaced by a new one describing what it looks like (spiny-leaved). It has been cultivated since at least the early seventeenth century, when it was described growing in the gardens of the Villa Farnese in Rome. The flowers are very pale green, small saucers held together on a very stout stem. In the wild it is found in a wide variety of situations – growing through scrub, on open hillsides, by the banks of streams – and it is equally tolerant of habitats in the garden. Brian Mathew, the great authority on hellebores, considers that the best plants will be those growing on deep, rich soil in full sun or only partial shade. In heavy shade the plant tends to become drawn and leggy and may start to lean, or worse, fall completely at the first serious puff of wind. Because it is such a stiff, unyielding plant, it can do nothing by halves and any collapse will be total.

If you are fitting this March scheme into a small space, you will have to choose between the hellebore and the darker-leaved spurge, *Euphorbia amygloides robbiae*, which is less sculptural, less august, more of an opportunist. It is deeply subdued for most of the year, with leathery whorls of leaves carried at the end of woody stems. In spring it carries bright yellow-green heads of flowers above the leaves. It spreads by underground shoots and tends to wander off in directions rather different from the ones you had in mind, dying out in the spot where you originally planted it. It is not so good that you would lead anyone on a pilgrimage to see it, the way you do with a wisteria or a patch of lilies, but a garden cannot be made entirely of stars : they would keep stealing each other's thunder. The euphorbia has no ideas above its station and its wayward habits sometimes give you pleasant surprises, as when it pokes through a crack in paving where you could never have planted it, or bobs up among a bed of daffodils, which are brilliant both with the sombre green of the leaves and with the lime tones of the flower head. It will do the same for forsythia, the dark foliage lending substance to the shrub's flowers on their bare stems.

Either blue *Anemone blanda* or fat blue Dutch crocus would make a fine carpet under this March group. The anemones have dissected ferny foliage and many-petalled daisy flowers in blue, white and pink. For this scheme, the blue is best. The usual way to plant them is as dried tubers in autumn, but if you forget, you can indulge in some satisfying instant gardening, by buying potfuls of plants in bud towards the end of February and planting them out, with plenty of compost or leaf-mould round them. Like many spring bulbs, they are ideal for places underneath deciduous shrubs. In early spring, when they most need it, they are in full sun. In summer when the shrub comes into leaf, they get some shade. If they are happy, they will seed themselves about, but this is only likely to happen if they are left undisturbed. Where there are dogs and children, this rarely happens. The anemones have a slightly wistful quality. The crocuses are quite the reverse, like small apoplectic old men, keeling over suddenly after an excess of port wine. They are much showier than the anemones, right for the forsythia, possibly too much for the corylopsis which would prefer to do its palely loitering act with the languishing anemones. The big crocus are an excellent antidote for gardeners who are in danger of vanishing altogether in their own refinement. Although birds do not attack purple crocus in the same way as they do yellow ones, mice are less discriminating and munch on bulbs of all colours. This is not a new problem. Engravings of crocus in the *Hortus Floridus* published in Utrecht in 1614 include one of a mouse feasting on a crocus corm. E. A. Bowles, the famous Edwardian gardener who wrote a classic quartet of books, *My Garden in Spring* and so on, was a crocus fiend and consequently a psychopath where mice were concerned. 'Mice need fighting in all months and by any means,' he wrote and went on to recommend a complicated armoury of traps baited with Brazil nuts, cats, poison and slippery jars sunk in the ground. He had some no-nonsense ways with birds and caterpillars as well. But this was a man who was prepared to wait thirty years before his cross-fertilization programme produced a pure white seedling of the Greek species *C. sieberi*. Such dedication excuses a certain paranoia.

Do not get taken in by the optimistic writers of bulb catalogues who describe some crocus as blue. They are all lighter or darker shades of purple. 'Remembrance', nearly always described as a rich blue, is actually a deep mauve. But it is still an outstanding crocus, as is 'Purpureus Grandiflorus' and the paler 'Queen of the Blues', refined lavender. None of these big Dutch crocuses was refined enough for Bowles, however. He called them gamps and compared them unfavourably with the species such as *C. tomasinianus* which, as they come up, have the elegant, tightly furled look of brand new umbrellas. These will be too early for this March scheme, but you can easily tuck some into a corner to produce colour earlier in the year.

Magnolia stars

For a final, simple March scheme in white, pink and blue, choose the early magnolia *M. stellata* and carpet it underneath with clumps of hairy-leaved lungwort (pulmonaria) and drifts of bright blue scilla or the similar chionodoxa. There is nothing more magnificent in suburban gardens than the sudden explosion in spring of magnolias, usually the type with goblet flowers balanced along the stems. *M. stellata* is less spectacular, but quicker, flowering at quite a precocious age, usually no more than two years after planting. You must wait at least five years for the big Soulangeanas to perform. The stellata's flowers are strappy, like a badly tied bow, quite unlike the waxy chalices of the big magnolias, and it will scarcely be more than 5ft/1.5m across after ten years' growing. It has no pretensions to be a fully fledged tree. The flowers open from promisingly fat, furry buds and like the bigger magnolias, it blooms before the leaves emerge, which throws the flowers into greater prominence than they would otherwise have. They smell good. So does the wood, if you prune off a dead stem : it smells spicy, like cloves. Find a position sheltered from north and east winds which will burn the flower buds. There are pink varieties, such as 'King Rose' and 'Rosea', but the white has more punch. There is also a variety called 'Water Lily' which has larger flowers with more petals than the ordinary type, but it has not proved to be such a strong or reliable shrub as its parent.

Either the pink or the white will be complemented by mounds of lungwort. This month they are concentrating on producing their flowers, which drift indeterminately in many varieties from pink to blue. Later they turn to leaf production and these, large, hairy and mottled with silver, provide excellent ground cover during the summer. In this way, the variegated pulmonarias are much better value than types such as 'Munstead Blue' which have coarse green leaves, though flowers of a piercing azure in spring. The term 'ground cover' is often used in rather a despairing way, as though it were a last resort, like linoleum in the bathroom. Well used, it can become the most interesting part of any planting scheme. Ground cover sounds baldly utilitarian, but plants used for this purpose can not only cover ground, they can be knitted into groups of different colours and textures, which each year, as plants ebb and flow, will have a slightly different effect. Good ground cover can be as rich as a Persian carpet. It may also suppress weeds, but you should not think of it only in this policing role. Primarily it should be there to give pleasure. Pulmonaria, as it happens, is an extremely effective smotherer of annual weeds, as its leaves start to grow at the same time as weeds and soon overlay them. (No ground cover will get the better of deeply rooted perennial weeds, such as ground elder, horsetail, bindweed or couch.) The best leaves belong to *P. saccharata*. They are up to 12in/30cm long, dark green generously marbled with silver, and very rough to the touch. It likes a cool, rich soil in light shade, which the magnolia will give it when it comes into leaf, but tolerates a wide range of homes. *P. longifolia* has distinctive lance-shaped leaves, much thinner than other types. They hug the ground more closely than those of other varieties and the flowers are a brighter blue. There are some with leaves almost entirely washed with silver, such as *P. saccharata argentea* and *P. vallarsae* 'Margery Fish'.

Among the clumps of pulmonaria use quantities of small bulbs, not five or ten of a kind, but twenty or thirty. They are one of the greatest joys of March and provide as pleasant a way to bankrupt yourself as any other – so much better for your liver than food or drink. Scillas immediately come to mind for this scheme, but it could equally well be puschkinias or chionodoxas. Scillas make themselves at home very easily and have neat foliage, much less bossy than their relatives, our native bluebells. *S. bifolia* is an intense, bright blue, *S. siberica* a slightly later variety with sky-blue flowers. 'Spring Beauty' is taller (6in/15cm) and has the pale rather than the bright blue flowers. All are lovely. They are easy to establish and rather better garden guests than grape hyacinths, which have too high a proportion of leaf to flower. Specialist suppliers list some extremely choice species, such as *S. peruviana* and *S. rosenii*, which flowers much later in May with reflexed flowers of white and blue. Once you lose your heart to these, or to *S. greilhuberi* with petals of greyish blue and white stamens topped with knobs of brilliant blue

1 *Magnolia stellata*

DECIDUOUS SHRUB
HEIGHT AND SPREAD
5 X 6FT/1.5 X 1.8M
ZONE 5—9

Scented white strap-petalled flowers
are carried through March and April.
Magnolias get their name from an
early eighteenth century French pro-
fessor of botany, Pierre Magnol. *Stellata* describes the flowers, not
cup-shaped like others of this
tribe, but wide open floppy stars.
This is a Japanese species brought
over to England in Victorian
times. The bark is aromatic
and the flowers too have a rich
sweet scent. The variety called
'Water Lily' has large flowers with
more petals than the standard type,
but it does not have such a robust constitution. The shrub is slow-growing,
but tolerant of a wide variety of soils
except those that are extremely alkaline. Plant in spring in full sun or light
shade, avoiding places where
early sun may fall on
frosted buds. No regular
pruning is needed. Top-
dress each spring with leaf-
mould or compost. Propagate either
by cuttings of half-ripe wood in July
or by layering low branches in spring.

2 Pulmonaria (Lungwort)
DECIDUOUS PERENNIAL
HEIGHT AND SPREAD
12 X 18IN/30 X 45CM
ZONE 4–8

These are strong-growing plants, in full leaf between April and November. Flowers, in various shades of pink and blue, are borne on stems backed by small leaves during early spring. The showiest are those with variegated leaves. In this scheme, avoid *Pulmonaria rubra* with plain leaves and brick red flowers. Look instead for forms of *P. saccharata* with handsome leaves heavily blotched with silver-grey. 'Argentea' has leaves that are almost covered in silver. If you want flowers that contrast with the scilla's brilliant blue, choose pulmonarias with pinkish rather than bluish flowers. Plant from October to March in any decent garden soil. Leafy plants such as these need plenty of nitrogen, so mulch liberally in early spring to provide food and conserve moisture at the roots. Propagate by dividing plants in autumn or spring.

3 Scilla
BULB
HEIGHT AND SPREAD
6 X 4IN/15 X 10CM
ZONE 5–9

Scillas will grow anywhere except in the driest and dustiest of soils. They are as happy in part shade as in sun. *Scilla siberica* will find anywhere in a British garden like the Ritz Hotel after life in its native Siberia. 'Spring Beauty' has very intense blue flowers, but if you want an all white picture – rather a waste of the scilla – there is an albino called 'Alba'. *S. bifolia* is equally easy to grow, sometimes a scrap taller than its cousin. Its leaves

wait half-developed until the flowers begin to fade before they finish growing. Plant them about 3in/7.5cm deep and, if you remember, mulch them with leaf-mould or sifted compost in the autumn. They self-seed liberally and look particularly pretty when they stray on to gravel paths beside beds. They poke their heads through gravel with no problem; concrete would probably fox them.

4 Leucojum vernum (Snowflake)
BULB
HEIGHT AND SPREAD
8 × 4IN/20 × 10cm
ZONE 5–9

These are related to snowdrops and for March *L. vernum* is the one to choose. *L. aestivum* does not appear until April. Bulbs are usually on sale in autumn and should be planted as soon as you can get hold of them. They like moist soils which do not bake in summer, but do not want deep shade. Mix compost and bonemeal into the soil at planting time.

turquoise pollen, you are done for. They are generally more difficult to grow, however, and are specialities for troughs and screes. For mass planting, stick to the excellent and cheap common types. You can get twenty *S. siberica* for the price of one of the more abstruse species, gorgeous though they are. Chionodoxa is closely related to scilla, but if you look at the stamens, you see that those of chionodoxa are all held together, while those of scilla fan out separately. In the garden they like the same conditions and are equally good in half shade. *C. sardensis* is pale blue with a white eye, interesting but not as telling as the scillas. The puschkinia is another close relative. *P. libanotica* has very pale blue flowers, held round the stem like a small hyacinth. For a more ethereal effect use a scattering of white bulbs too, using perhaps the snowflake *Leucojum vernum*. They are related to snowdrops, but their flowers have six equal petals, rather than three outer and three inner as the snowdrops do. The white bells are tipped with green. Later on you could create a diversionary sideshow for the autumn, by planting autumn crocus among the pulmonarias.

APRIL

T. S. ELIOT'S APRIL WAS 'THE CRUELLEST MONTH, BREEDING/LILACS out of the dead land.' For gardeners it is not so much cruel as capricious, a see-saw of extremes, in which a blazingly sunny day with temperatures around 70°F/ 20°C can be followed by a stiff ground frost. Out of blue skies there can come snowstorms of astonishing ferocity, laying low daffodils and with them the visions of the impatient gardener. By April, we have had enough of winter, enough of gardening by proxy in books and nursery catalogues and want deep, undiluted draughts of the real thing. April usually marks the beginning of the stampede towards the yellow posters of the National Gardens Scheme. Garden visiting is now as competitive a sport as birdwatching has become. We have grubbers as well as twitchers. By Easter, country lanes are full of their cars, lurching uncertainly through the navigational ballet that this particular sport demands. 'First left, second right, over the hump-backed bridge, third left after the church. No, no, NO! I said *third* left.' There are tears and recriminations throughout the land, as the map runs out, the rain closes in and the garden to visit, like Brigadoon, retreats into an impenetrable maze of mist and rotten signposting. There is a corresponding rush to the garden centres of the land as dreams of Nirvana awaken in Balham. April is the month not of Eliot's lilac, which flowers in May and June, but of the classic woodland plants – the big magnolias, early rhododendrons, pieris – brought back by plant hunters in the nineteenth century from the Himalayas and China. It is, in many ways, their misfortune that they all look so come-hitherish in their neat containers in the garden centre. Anxious for a palpable message that the worst of the year is indeed behind them, novice gardeners fall, like travellers at an oasis, on plants such as the rhododendrons which are in flower now, bear them home in triumph and then, as often as not, stuff them into sticky clay, pulsating with pH numbers, in a measly hole which is all they can dig before it is time for tea.

These woodland plants like woodland conditions: cool, moist, peaty and, above all, acid ground. Unless you have the right kind of soil there is no point in planning your own minute version of the great woodland gardens of Cornwall and the west coast of Scotland. It is not chance that dictates the position of these gardens, but geology and meteorology. Before you get carried away with the notion of a grove of rhododendrons glowing in a shady corner as your chosen contribution to the April scene, check your soil. Rhododendrons do best where the soil is between 4.5 and 6.0pH. Climate has a part to play as well. The west coast of Britain generally gets wetter summers and warmer winters than the east. This maddens holidaymakers who go there in summer, but pleases rhododendrons very much indeed. They can hardly be expected to flourish in situations where they are baked in full sun all summer and whipped by freezing easterly winds in winter.

Magnolias are slightly less picky than rhododendrons and pieris, another classic shrub of the big woodland gardens. All they ask is a lime-free soil, not a specifically acid one. Woodlanders such as rhododendrons can be used in tubs in shady courtyards, as they have compact rootballs that adapt with little complaint to life in restricted circumstances. Look particularly for some of the early-flowering scented rhododendrons such as *R.* 'Fragrantissimum'. By Christmas you will already be able to count the number of flower buds swelling inside their ruffs of dark evergreen leaves. As spring arrives, the flower buds explode into clusters of huge white trumpets, flushed with pink. They not only look spectacular, but smell as rich as summer, as heady as muscat wine. 'Lady Alice Fitzwilliam' is similarly scented but has yellow rather than pink staining the petals. The old Victorian varieties 'Countess of Haddington' and pink 'Princess Alice' are equally lovely. They were bred as cool conservatory plants and are not reliably hardy, but any slight *Angst* that this might cause is more than repaid by the sight and smell of them where they do flourish. They have a characteristically rangy habit of growth, but will take a long time to reach 5ft/1.5m in any direction.

Magnolias are spectacular flowering shrubs this month as they throw off the furry wraps round their buds to reveal the fleshy flowers inside. They are dramatic in outline and in the way that they hold their goblet-shaped flowers on bare leafless branches. The great aristocrats are the forest-sized species such as *M. campbellii*. Ordinary mortals will be content with one of the varieties of *M. x soulangeana* that rarely exceeds 10ft/3m at maturity. White flowers, stained rosy purple at the base, open out in warm weather from cups into saucers, about 6in/15cm across. For impact, there is little to beat the white flowers, but those who like their effects more muted may prefer 'Lennei' with rounded rose-purple flowers. Magnolias are so splendid, like old-fashioned epergnes displaying their blossoms, that they need no distraction, perhaps just a carpet of bulbs round their feet. If you have not used a magnolia in your March planting scheme, think of using one now, with a large group of tulips that hold their flowers in the same stiff-necked way as the magnolias do. Grey 'Spring Pearl' with vermilion edging would do where you wanted a cool recessive picture, 'Van der Neer', a rich purple-mauve, if you wanted to pick up the wine-coloured staining on the base of the magnolia petals.

Bulbs are, of course, an indispensable part of spring planting. Crowds of daffodils burst upon gardens now and there are other newcomers : hyacinths, fritillaries and leucojum. The best thing about bulbs is that so often you forget you have planted them. Then, suddenly in spring, there they are, not the slightest bit put out that you have not been worrying over them or making them special snacks. There is a black side to this, of course: there always is. It is the mortifying experience of spearing a dormant bulb through the heart on the end of your gardening fork. All you can do is to apologize profusely and rebury the stricken bulb tenderly with some special compost to soothe the wound. They do not lend themselves to instant gardening. You can buy them already growing in pots in spring, but at a price. You may succumb to some potted specialities, the narcissus 'Minnow' or some species tulips, but a good spring display will require six months' forethought and a planting session in September or October, as soon as you can get hold of the bulbs.

Daffodils are pre-eminent in April, but choosing varieties among the ever-increasing lists is a difficult business. The whole family has been divided into classes, twelve of them, according to flower type : large or small cup, split, double or trumpet. The niceties matter more to those who breed and show than they do to ordinary gardeners, but since most daffodil lists are now arranged in divisions, it helps to have a vague idea of the types you most like. The monsters are in divisions one and two. Division ten holds the wild species, the elegant *Narcissus poeticus* with white petals and flat bright red frilly cups, and the wild daffodil *N. pseudonarcissus*. This has papery white petals and a lemon-yellow trumpet. This division also includes the brilliant little wild jonquil, *N. jonquilla*, only 10in/25cm high, with grassy foliage and bright golden flowers, quite staggeringly scented.

Other miniatures can be used in alpine gardens, in an open pocket in a rockery, or a shallow stone trough, woven together with tiny botanical tulips, the strikingly variegated foliage of arabis, *A. caucasica* 'Variegata', and the silky, deeply dissected foliage of the Pasque flower, *Pulsatilla vulgaris*. It would be foolhardy to go so far as to say this is an alpine collection. True alpine gardeners would pass over such kindergarten stuff as arabis and species daffodils. They warm to the fiendishly difficult things that need months in the refrigerator before they will germinate. They swap horror stories about their charges, as parents do about their children. 'Well, I tried *everything* and the only thing that worked was . . .' and then they are off into realms of esotericism that make freemasonry seem as simple as ring-a-roses. But, if you have not already been drawn into the magnificently besotted ranks of the Alpine Garden Society, or are rather a tentative novice in the whole business of gardening, plants such as arabis have the advantage of being good, tough stayers. The plain variety romps away like a weed and would soon smother delicate neighbours. The variegated version is more tentative in its approaches, but very eye-catching with its rosettes of leaves, heavily edged with cream and sprays of white flowers. The Pasque flower is not quite so easy-going. In the wild, it chooses chalky, well-drained slopes in full sun and these are the conditions that you must try and reproduce in the garden. This does not mean hacking pieces out of the South Downs to bring back to your plot. General principles are the thing : no shade, no damp, no acidity. Sharp drainage is the real key. If you get this right, the plant will reward you with masses of ferny foliage, at most 12in/30cm high, followed in April and May by rich, cup-shaped flowers, usually purple, all with a brilliant boss of gold stamens. The buds have an extraordinary silky sheen and the seed-heads, too, have the ghostly evanescence of old man's beard. The common one is lovely, but there are named varieties. 'Mrs van der Elst' is pale pink and 'Rubra' red. Parkinson, who gardened in Long Acre, now at the middle of London's Covent Garden, did rather better in the seventeenth century for he mentioned a yellow as well as a red and a white Pasque flower. No one has seen it since. For yellow, we must return to bulbs – no hardship.

Bulbs have the huge advantage of tidying themselves away completely for the second half of the year and leaving the ground clear for a new scheme. In a small trough you can plant miniature hebe or penstemon to fill the gap later in the year. In a border, if for instance you have used them in the earlier scheme, under japonica, they could be replaced by shaggy asters or groups of late-flowering *Salvia patens*. In a small spring group with arabis, the bulbs could be replaced by *Cyclamen hederifolium*, or by summer-flowering alliums, such as the brilliant blue *Allium caeruleum*. The little jonquil 'Baby Moon', no more than 7in/17.5cm high, bearing three or four brilliant yellow flowers on each stem, would be about the right scale for this present scheme, or the tiny trumpet daffodil *N. asturiensis* (syn. *N. minimus*), like a 'King Alfred' shrunk in the wash. It is only 6in/15cm high. The tulips can give you yellow, too. *T. tarda* is endearingly egg-coloured, yolk-yellow in the centre of the petals with white round the outer edges. It comes from central Asia, like so many of the botanical tulips, and has a flat rosette of narrow leaves from which come clusters of wide starry flowers, perhaps five to a stem, but no more than 6in/15cm tall. *T. chrysantha* also has a yellow flower, but the outside of the petals is flushed with red. It grows about 8in/20cm high, the blooms held on elegantly slender stems.

A group of extroverts

For an extrovert April scheme of brilliant yellow and red, intolerable to a melancholy poet such as Eliot, combine a good clear-coloured japonica such as *Chaenomeles x superba* 'Crimson and Gold' with groups of daffodils and single early tulips. Use wallflowers as buffers, together with clumps of epimedium that will look good all year, long after the bulbs have disappeared below ground. For this scheme to work, you need to avoid japonicas with too much salmon in them and daffodils with too much lemon. *Chaenomeles* 'Crimson and Gold' is a clear deep red. The blood-coloured 'Rowallane' would also be suitable, or the deep crimson *C. speciosa* 'Sanguinea Plena'. In a mild winter, they may ruin your plans by flowering in January and February, but the textbooks assure you that March to May is the proper time : unfortunately japonicas don't read. If there is a wall to frame this April group, plant the chaenomeles against it and keep it well tied in, where it will make a stiff, angular framework, with the buds breaking open on bare dark stems, like a Japanese print. If you have no wall, it will be equally happy as the centrepiece of a group with the bulbs and other plants clustered round its feet.

For the daffodil, you need a variety that is a clear yellow, but less lumpen than old 'King Alfred'. 'Peeping Tom' is charming, but usually over too early for an April show, as are the rest of this Cyclamineus group, all of which have swept-back petals, as though they have been caught in a hurricane. 'Golden Ducat' is the right colour, a uniform, pure yellow, and flowers at the right time, but is double, which arouses deep prejudice in some otherwise perfectly liberal horticulturists. 'St Keverne' is a deep, clear golden yellow and very free flowering. The choice is easier if you study daffodils in the flesh, rather than reading about them in catalogues. Yellows are difficult to describe and can easily veer off into shades harsher than neon lights.

Size on its own will not necessarily make a good daffodil. The parts need to be well-proportioned with the right amount of cup or trumpet to petal and a stem that is the right height for the build of the flower. Strong stems are important in April when flowers must withstand sudden storms and wild winds. With the daffodils you need some tulips of an uncompromising Turkey red, not a difficult colour to find among this tribe. The Fosteriana tulip 'Cantata' is outstanding, with long, thin, pointed vermilion buds that open out into blazing flowers with pointed petals. The colour is clean and bright and the leaves, not often a great asset with tulips, are bright green and as glossy as an

1 *Chaenomeles x superba* 'Crimson and Gold' (Japonica, cydonia)

DECIDUOUS SHRUB
HEIGHT AND SPREAD
6 x 6 FT/1.8 x 1.8 M
ZONE 6—9

This may begin flowering in January, but generally continues through April. Bowl-shaped flowers of waxy texture are held close to the dark twigs. They thrive in any soil, in sun or part shade. Flowering will be more prolific in sun. Plant in autumn or spring and

mulch every year to keep its spirits up. If grown against a wall, prune after flowering in May by cutting back all the new growth to two or three buds. Propagate by cuttings taken with a heel in July and August.

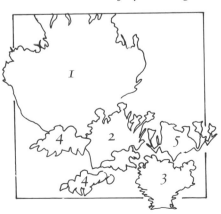

2 *Narcissus* (Daffodil)

BULB
HEIGHT AND SPREAD
VARIES ACCORDING TO
SPECIES
ZONE 6—8

These are the most popular of springtime bulbs, flowering in a broad swathe from late February through to the middle of May, though dates vary considerably according to the region. Most narcissus are hardy, but some types such as 'Paper White' and 'Soleil d'Or' grow outside only in the extreme southwest. The International Register kept by the Royal Horticultural Society has 8000 different varieties on it. Most are undemanding. Triandrus hybrids ('Thalia', 'Liberty Bells') prefer warm, well-drained situations, as do the jonquils ('Trevithian', 'Suzy'). Tazetta types, such as 'Cheerfulness', need a good baking in summer if they are to thrive. Otherwise, plant daffodils in August and September, setting the bulbs at least 6in/15cm deep. This way, you will not disturb them when you are trowelling around in summer. Give them some bonemeal at planting time. Split clumps in summer.

APRIL · Scheme 1
A group of extroverts

3 *Cheiranthus cheiri* (Wallflower)

EVERGREEN PERENNIAL, used as a biennial

HEIGHT AND SPREAD

12 X 12IN/30 X 30CM

ZONE 6–9

For the planting scheme with chaenomeles and daffodils, a deep, tawny-red wallflower will be the best choice, perhaps 'Blood Red' or 'Fire King'. 'Vulcan' is a deep velvety crimson. Sow seed in a well-prepared seedbed in late May or early June. Transplant the seedlings about 12in/ 30cm apart. Pinch out the tops when they have recovered from the transplanting. Set out in their flowering positions in September.

4 *Epimedium* (Barrenwort)

EVERGREEN AND DECIDUOUS PERENNIALS

HEIGHT AND SPREAD

12 X 12IN/30 X 30CM

ZONE 5–9

The leaves of these ground-covering plants are rather more important than the flowers. All the family are ornamental plants, the deciduous ones daintier than evergreen E. *perralderianum* with its sprays of yellow flowers in June. Earliest to flower are the deciduous E. *x warleyense* with

prickly green leaves and coppery flowers in April and May and E. *x youngianum* with mid-green leaves marked with red and small pink flowers in April and May. 'Niveum' is a white-flowered form. Plant in autumn or spring in moist soil. They grow most happily in half shade but will be content with sun, provided they do not dry out. Top-dress with compost in early spring and shear off old foliage before the flowers appear. Propagate by dividing in autumn or spring.

5 *Tulip*

BULB

HEIGHT AND SPREAD

ACCORDING TO VARIETY

ZONE 5–9

Tulip bulbs should not be planted before November as new growth induced by early planting may be subject to frost. Lord Mayor's Day is the traditional time, but if the ground remains workable, neither soggy nor frostbound, they can be pushed in any time up until Christmas. Flowering will then be slightly delayed. A sprinkling of bonemeal in each hole will help them on their way. A dibber is not the best tool to use for making holes. They are generally not big enough for the tulip to sit in comfortably and the pointed end of the dibber often leaves a gap under the bulb where earth should be. Use a trowel and excavate a decent home for the bulb if you want it to do its best. They thrive in alkaline soils. Add lime to heavy acid ground before planting. Dead-head the flowers when the petals fall but leave the stem and foliage to feed the bulb below.

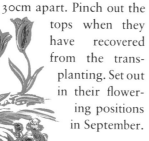

arum's. The single early 'Keizerskroon', bright crimson scarlet deeply edged with yellow, is slightly taller and slightly later to flower. There are few duds among tulips and one of the great delights of bulbs is that you can try different combinations each season. The daffodils, once planted, will be more likely to reappear than the tulips.

If you have room, fill in between groups of bulbs with epimedium, either *E. perralderianum* or *E. pinnatum* which will give bulk to the ground-level planting and provide cover long after the bulbs have gone. The leaves are tough and lopsidedly heart-shaped as a begonia's are. They are held on wiry stems. Enthusiastic gardeners warble about marvellous bronze tints on the leaves of the evergreen species during the winter. More jaundiced souls grumble that they look half dead. All of them have tiny flowers, very delicate, which will make little impact unless you remember to trim away old foliage in February before they emerge.

Wallflowers are an indispensable part of an April garden and can be tucked into any spaces left on the ground floor of this group. The *Oxford English Dictionary* tells you when the word acquired its pejorative, left-on-the-sidelines meaning (the poet Winthrop Praed in 'County Ball' 1820: 'The maiden wallflowers of the room . . .'), but not why. However it happened, it is a calumny. Although they are often badly used, wallflowers are never hackneyed. The rich tawny colours are natural companions for both daffodils and tulips and the smell, when a warmish shaft of sun tickles their scent glands, a glorious antidote to the sloth brought on by winter hibernation. If you have no room for them with the japonica and bulbs, use them in tubs close to the door that you most often use where you can smell them every time you come outside. It has been another of the plant's burdens always to have been part of rent-a-crowd, never a solo star. One wallflower is a ludicrous proposition. Daffodils, which suffer from the same difficulty, at least had a poem written about them. You also have to use wallflowers *en masse*. They are not in themselves beautiful objects, though if you have room to allow them to become the perennials that they are by nature, rather than ripping them from the ground when they have finished flowering, they develop into rather venerable, sprawling plants, good when seen flopping over the edge of a raised terrace bed, or best of all, out of a crack in a stone wall. If badly grown, they are leggy, scraggy things, but they have the potential to be outstanding. There is that smell, and a wonderfully subfusc range of colours, rich mahogany as well as pale cream, dirty purple and glowing ruby. There is a seed mixture called 'Persian Carpet' which exactly describes the effect. You can also get separate colours.

The cheapest way to get them is to grow your own and these are likely to be twice as good as any that you see for sale in autumn, stacked mournfully in bundles of a dozen in buckets on market stalls. The seed should be sown some time between late May and the middle of June. It does not hang around long before germinating. Then you must see that the plants grow lustily and without check (give them plenty of water) to get them past the dangerous juvenile stage when they are most attractive to the flea beetle. This is a small blackish creature, no more than a quarter of an inch/6mm long, that hops like a joke-shop frog when you disturb it. It munches irritating holes in the young leaves of wallflowers and other members of the cabbage tribe. This is rarely fatal, but can be debilitating. After this initial sowing, there are two good things you can do that commercial growers rarely do. You can transplant the seedlings, setting them 12in/30cm apart, so each has plenty of room to develop. July is usually the right time for this job, if you have sown seed in May. You can also remember to pinch out the tops of the little plants when they are no more than 4–5in/10–12cm high. This will encourage them to make bushy, vigorous growth with more than one flowering head on each plant. In autumn, lift each plant with a trowel so that plenty of earth hangs around the roots and plant it into its final home. They will not do any more growing, so to get the best display, set them hugger-mugger. If you are using them with bulbs, plant wallflowers first, bulbs after. Then you will not accidentally spear bulbs hidden underground.

Space is the biggest difficulty if you grow your own. You can line them out in a vegetable patch, but they will take up space for five months before they are planted out. If you do not have any spare ground, you will have to buy plants. Remember that what you buy in autumn is what you will see in April. If you buy measly plants, they will still be measly, though in flower in spring : no extra growing takes place during winter. Look for plants that have rounded well-developed heads of foliage rather than single stems and get them into the ground as soon as you can. Height depends to a certain extent on variety. Standard wallflowers grow to about 18in/45cm, but there are various dwarf strains with names such as 'Tom Thumb' that are considerably shorter and useful if you are trying to get the essence of the season in the space of a windowbox.

When wallflowers first came into this country, nobody knows. One authority suggests that it might have been at the time of the Norman conquest, on stone that was being hauled over from Normandy to build castles in England. John Gerard certainly knew them and in 1597 was writing that a double form 'groweth in most gardens of England.' Along with stocks and sweet williams, they became archetypal cottage-garden plants. The bedding craze of the nineteenth century brought them into grander homes, but they have never been looked on as smart plants. Today's plant snobs may spurn 'Persian

Carpet' and its kind and instead search out plants of 'Bloody Warrior' with ox-blood red double flowers set rather far apart on the stem. The special wallflowers 'Bloody Warrior', 'Harpur Crewe' (a double yellow), 'Baden-Powell' (smaller, but otherwise much the same) and the wallflower-like erysimum 'Bowles's Mauve' (blue-grey foliage and soft purple flowers) are later to come into flower than the common sorts grown from seed which flower from April to June. The specialities won't start until May.

An explosion of blossom

Cherries are also stalwarts of the April scene, for spring – which started on the ground in March with crocuses and primroses – creeps up into the trees now and sets off soft explosions of blossom. The choice of cherries is enormous. Size may be the limiting factor. However taken you are with a tree in the garden centre, check what its eventual size is likely to be before you buy. The wild gean, *Prunus avium*, especially in its double form 'Plena', is one of the loveliest of all flowering cherries, but it grows to formidable proportions, perhaps 40ft/12m high and 30ft/9m wide. That could be an entire front garden swallowed up and the sitting-room windows pushed in as well. The popular 'Kanzan' is an unpromising pink, the colour of icing packed with E numbers. It is also a vigorous grower, getting to 30ft/9m in height, 25ft/7.5m across. Choice of colour is an entirely personal matter, but the softer pinks and white are easier to work into mixed plantings than deeply disturbing pinks. 'Amanogawa' looks promising, with its upright growth and pale pink flowers, but these are likely to be too late for an April display and the habit of growth, charming in youth, becomes ungainly in age. 'Hally Jolivette' is a better proposition, neat in growth, not more than 20ft/6m in any direction, with willowy branches covered in semi-double white flowers that continue through April and May. 'Tai Haku' is superb with clusters of big white flowers contrasting with the bronze of the young leaves in April, but it is big. It reaches 30ft/9m and spreads almost as much, but where there is room for it, this is the finest cherry of all this month. 'Ukon' brings a completely different colour into the cherry spectrum with semi-double flowers of cream and palest yellow tinged with green which emerge among bronze-purple leaves. It grows to about 20ft/6m and spreads to the same extent.

Any of these – or an amelanchier – can fill the centre of a planting scheme for an April wasteland. Blue, pink and purple predominate with a dark evergreen osmanthus – sweetly scented – taking over the middle ground at the edge of the tree's canopy. Dicentra, wood anemones, fritillaries and bright blue omphalodes fill in at ground level. There is some confusion in the labelling of amelanchier. You may find identical plants in different garden centres labelled as *A. canadensis, A. laevis* or *A. lamarckii* and available as a many-branched shrub or a small tree. Buying a tree will give you more room to play with underneath, as the canopy is light and airy. Whichever name you buy it under, the tree you want has oval, bronze young leaves that sometimes have good red and yellow tints in autumn and sprays of white flowers. Besides the autumn colour, a trick that not all cherries can match, the advantage of amelanchier over cherry in certain situations is its delicacy. It is smaller in all its parts which can be an advantage.

Under the tree you might like to create a simple, low-level carpet of bulbs and ground cover, punctuated with some stands of taller-growing honesty, which will furnish the patch in winter with bleached discs of papery seed-heads. If you want more bulk in the planting, use the handsome, restrained, but usefully evergreen shrub *Osmanthus delavayi*, which has neat, glossy leaves, sharply toothed, and clusters of scented tubular white flowers in April and May. It is slow, but classy. Dicentra could be used as part of the understorey. Three of the family have grey, glaucous leaves as fretted as a fern's, which are a pleasure to have in the garden, even when there are none of the bleeding heart flowers to go with them. The roots are brittle, so plant them with care in a good rich patch of soil. The flowers will not come until May and June. *Anemone nemorosa*, the windflower or wood anemone, will thrive in the shadiest area you can find under the amelanchier or cherry. The corms are sometimes difficult to establish, but once happy, the flowers will seed themselves about liberally. They are as fragile as tissue, white in the common variety, pale lavender in the form called 'Robinsoniana'. If there is no ground that seems shady and woodlandy enough for the anemones, think instead of the snakeshead fritillaries, *Fritillaria meleagris*, which like a more open situation, as long as it is damp. Although now rare in the wild, they are not at all difficult to establish in the garden. They do not like to be chivvied, so if they decide that they like you and flower in their strange, angular, spotted way, leave well alone. There are purple and white flowers and the leaves are thin and grassy. There is a kind of fragile sadness about both anemones and fritillaries that you may feel is inappropriate for the new beginnings that April portends. Anemones can be cheered up with erythroniums, which enjoy the same cool, shady conditions. 'White Beauty' would be just the thing with the pale blue 'Robinsoniana' anemone, or pale sulphur 'Pagoda', which exactly describes what the flower looks like, with plain white anemones. The snakesheads are so bizarre that they need no company but the feathery dicentra foliage. If you find all yours come up purple, lighten the effect with a few groups of specially ordered 'Alba', which is white with green veining, or 'Aphrodite', which is pure white.

1 *Prunus* (Cherry)
DECIDUOUS TREE
HEIGHT AND SPREAD
VARIES WITH SPECIES
ZONE 6–9

'Kanzan', overplanted in suburban streets all over the country, has put some people off cherries for life, but a cure may be effected by planting one of the more ethereal varieties instead. Some colour well in autumn. They are shallow-rooting, so do not cultivate the soil too deeply round their feet. Plant in autumn and stake if the site is exposed or windy. No

regular pruning is needed, but if you want to cut out a branch, do it in late summer. Mulch regularly in autumn or spring. Named varieties can only be propagated by buds or grafts.

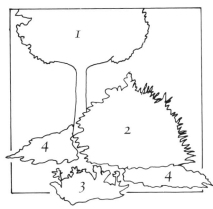

APRIL · Scheme 2
An explosion of blossom

2 Osmanthus delavayi

EVERGREEN SHRUB
HEIGHT AND SPREAD
6 x 6FT/1.8 x 1.8M
ZONE 7–10

Restrained, compact and slow growing, this is not a showy shrub, but one that at first you take for granted and then come to depend upon. If box seems to you a waste of space, use osmanthus instead, discreetly clipped into a neat, rounded shape. The leaves are pointed and the long, tubular white flowers heavily scented. Plant in sun or half shade in any decent garden soil between autumn and spring. Mulch annually. Propagate by cuttings of half-ripe shoots taken in July. If you do not intend to shape it, no regular pruning is required. Its name comes from the Greek *osme*, meaning fragrance, its salient characteristic. O. *x burkwoodi* is similarly spring flowering, and has O. *delavayi* as one of its parents. Osmanthus is generally hardy but may be prone to leaf scorch in very cold, windy winters.

3 Erythronium (Dog's tooth violet)

TUBER
HEIGHT AND SPREAD
6 x 12IN/15 x 30CM
ZONE 5–9

The common name comes from the extraordinary, elongated tubers which look like canine teeth. *E. dens-canis* grows wild in southern Europe and Turkey, but there are several showier garden varieties available, such as 'White Splendour.' The flowers are graceful, with reflexed petals swept back over the top

of protruding stamens. The leaves are often marbled in grey or maroon. The general effect is of a small, delicate Turk's cap lily, the flowers no more than 2–3in across. The hybrid 'Pagoda' is much bigger than the species. It has striking sulphur-yellow flowers, marked with a central brown ring. The leaves are bronze. All like to be deeply planted in rich, moist soil which does not dry out. They are usually available in late summer. Once established leave them alone.

4 Anemone nemorosa (Windflower, wood anemone)

DECIDUOUS RHIZOME
HEIGHT AND SPREAD
6 x 6IN/15 x 15CM
ZONE 7–9

There are single and double, white, pink, mauve and blue forms of this fragile flower, a British native. You can learn what it needs in the garden by observing where it puts itself in the wild – usually deciduous woodlands, not on markedly acid soil. 'Robinsoniana' is a fine blue-lavender variety. It is not robust enough to fend off potential invaders, so keep the ground around its twiggy rhizomes clear. Plant in September or October in a cool, well-drained soil enriched with leaf-mould or, failing that, peat mixed with some bonemeal. A lightly shaded site that does not bake in summer will suit it best. Set the rhizomes about 2in/5cm below the ground. Alternatively, plant them in pots and set them out during the winter when they have already made roots. Propagate by seed sown during August and September.

MAY

ONLY THE MOST PROFESSIONAL PESSIMISTS CAN FAIL TO RESPOND TO May's special blend of recklessness and seduction. It is one of the few months in the year when, without screwing your eyes up too much, you can persuade yourself that the garden is looking good. The days are stretching out in an agreeable way, which usually leaves an hour before the sun goes down in the evening for a little wander in the greenery and some un-taxing snipping with secateurs. May is a relatively dry and sunny month, particularly in the southern half of the country. Gardeners in Scotland have to wait until June before temperatures warm up to southern England's Maytime peaks. May is a watershed in the garden, for once this month is past, tender plants such as geraniums and fuchsias, felicias and salvias can be set outside once again and bedding plants brought out permanently from their greenhouse cocoons to take their chance in the real world.

There is a gratifying sense of freshness about May, too, that makes it one of the best of all months in the garden. Lawn mowing is still enough of a novelty to be done as often as it should be. Growth on plants is vigorous, with a richness in the green tones that has entirely gone later in the summer. Plants in May have not reached the stroppy, floppy stage that renders them intractable by August. Anyone with a particular weakness for trees in blossom (and no bullfinches) will revel in May. The pessimists will point out that blossom is a fleeting pleasure. 'It'll all be gone in a few days,' they gloat, and find nothing else to say about it except that it is a nuisance the way it sticks to the windscreen of the car. Pessimists will also be able to tell you exactly how many sudden frosts they can remember in May and all about the time the neighbour's dog sat on the tulips. Optimists, on the other hand, will be spoilt for choice in May planting schemes. Choisya, which looks handsome all year with its glossy evergreen foliage, cross-dresses in a froth of white flowers in May. Clematis come into their own. Wisteria blossoms break out from unpromising prisons of gnarled grey stem. The problem lies not in suggesting what to put in to a planting plan, but in agonizing over what must be left out.

Blossom is an essential ingredient, but where does one start among the vast array of apples and pears, medlars and quinces that erupt this month ? The smaller the garden, the more important it is to make the right choice, because this may be the only tree that you have room for. It is sensible to choose a tree that can pay its way through more than May ; one that, as well as blossom, provides good foliage or perhaps fruit, together with good autumn colour later in the year. April's ornamental cherries are very fetching, but most will leave you hungry in autumn. An apple or a pear is less frivolous but more generous. It is essential to find out how big a tree is likely to be when it is mature, or you will have to face the murderous prospect of cutting one down in its prime. Many winsome saplings potted up at the garden centre turn into territorial monsters once their roots hit real earth. Dwarfing rootstocks are supposed to solve the problem as far as fruit trees are concerned, but these bring their own problems. A dwarf rootstock needs exceptionally rich soil to sustain an adequate top hamper of growth and fruit. In the long run, it is probably wiser to single out trees that do not innately want to take over the world and grow them on a standard rootstock that will not be so fussy about position and soil.

'Cox's Orange Pippin', 'Golden Delicious' and the other apples that are most commonly ranged on supermarket shelves are not necessarily the best varieties to grow in your own garden. They will give you your May blossom, but to fruit well, many commercial varieties need as much chemical dosing as a malingering hypochondriac. 'Cox' is a superb apple, raised around 1825 by a retired brewer, Richard Cox, from Bermondsey. The tree on which it grows however is prone to canker, particularly in cold, damp areas of the country, and susceptible to scab and mildew. To get 'Cox' to grow well, you will have to be forever patrolling with a spray gun. It is rarely happy north of the Wash and, anywhere, fussy about what it has got its feet in. It also needs a pollinator. This is another complication to bear in mind. Many fruit trees need a mate if they are to set fruit. If you have room for only one tree, you have two options : first, and easiest, to plant a self-fertile variety which will grow and crop happily on its own; second, to scan the neighbourhood with a pair of binoculars and spy out whether there are other likely pollinators not more than a bee's hop away. There often are. 'Ellison's Orange' is a superb early autumn apple which can be picked from the middle of September and eaten straight from the tree. The blossom is elegant pale pink and the tree itself not usually more than about 12ft/3.6m across. The monsters to avoid in a small garden are the 'Bramley' cooker, 'Tydeman's Early Worcester', 'Herring's Pippin', 'Blenheim Orange' and 'Laxton's Superb' which all make large, spreading trees.

Low bushes and pyramids are the shapes usually recommended for fruit trees, but where an apple or pear is doing double duty as centrepiece of a planting scheme and kitchen cropper, it is often better to plant a half-standard instead. Half-standards make graceful trees and because you have 4–5ft/1.2–1.5m of clean stem before any branches start, are easy to plant under. When the tree is established and able to cope with some competition at ground level, the effect of the blossomed arms spreading out over the underplanting will be rather pleasing. Planting a half-standard is also a useful way to get height in a new and perhaps rather bare garden. If you want height rather than width, think about a pear for your May blossom. Pear growth tends to be naturally far more upright than an apple's and the blossom white rather than pink. Of course, fruit is more difficult to pick from a half-standard and spraying is impossible but the aesthetic considerations are far more important (you must persuade yourself) than these mere midge-bites of inconvenience.

If you have a fence or wall behind the May plot, the options increase. You could put in a trained tree – a cordon, espalier or fan – as a background to the planting instead of a central half-standard. All types of trained tree need constant vigilance, however, and constant worrying with secateurs. Summer pruning is a must and it is odd how the tree that confronts you in the garden as you stand, secateurs poised, never looks anything like the tree in the textbook that you have just consulted. The regular, geometric shapes of trained fruit trees can enhance the garden's design, however – if they are well kept. Parallel rows of slanting cordons are very pleasing to the eye, but the cordon is quite a wasteful way of growing apples if you are as interested in the eating as the looking.

Apples and pears are not the only providers of blossom for a May planting scheme, but plum blossom is less showy and a plum's sex life often more difficult to arrange than an apple's or a pear's. The cheerful 'Victoria' is easy, but makes a large and not particularly shapely tree. A medlar would be a much more interesting and ornamental choice of tree than a plum, though you have to be an extremely *recherché* gourmet to make out much of an edible case for the fruit, which are beautiful, russet-coloured things like enormous brown, round rose hips. These often hang on the branches after the leaves have fallen and look wonderfully bizarre, an illustration from a Grimm brothers' fairy-tale. The leaves are long and tough and sometimes colour russet and red in the autumn. The tree blossoms with large flat white single flowers, somewhat like a quince's, each sitting in the middle of a rosette of leaves. The tree never gets very tall, but spreads to make a wide mushroom shape, the branches angular and dense. The trunk, quite early on, acquires venerable vertical slits down the bark. The medlar is a tree of great character, but the growth is denser than that of apple or pear and any underplanting will therefore be in more shade.

A fruiting centrepiece

All in all, the pear is probably the easiest tree to work with, whether you use it as a central standard or as a trained fan on a wall. Use one as an anchor for a May scheme of white, lemon, lime and blue with mahogany or apricot tulips. The pear will give the blossom that is the quintessential feature of an early May garden, and since it is an upright grower, will not be too demanding of space. The wild pear, *Pyrus communis*, is a wonderful tree dressed overall in May, but would be too vigorous for a small garden and bears no fruit worth eating, though it has good red leaves in autumn. 'Marguerite Marillat' is less vigorous, making a very upright tree, no more than 8ft/2.4m across, with enormous golden fruit in September and red leaves as well. The pears are juicy, but not as good in flavour as 'Beurre Hardy'. You cannot have everything. If you decide to go for a trained pear tree, try the well-known 'Conference' or perhaps 'Durondcau', which ripens in late October and November when the leaves turn crimson around the russet fruit.

If you use your pear spread-eagled against a fence or wall at the back of the group, you will need to fill the middle with something else. Pyramids of honeysuckle or clematis will do very well, posh trellis pyramids if you feel you can live up to them, bean poles lashed together in a tripod if you are intimidated by expensive obelisks. The earliest of the May honeysuckles is the version of our wild hedgerow climber called 'Early Dutch' or, confusingly, 'Belgica'. For smell, particularly in the evening, when honeysuckles pull out all the stops to attract passing moths, it is unparalleled. This would lounge admirably on the pyramid. So would clematis, where the choice is even wider. Look for mid-season varieties such as *C. macropetala* which has bell-shaped flowers in two shades of blue. The May-flowering clematis need little or no pruning, which is obliging of them, but you will have to look all winter at an unprepossessing tangle of stem on the pyramid. If you have used the pear in the centre of the group you could put a *Cornus alba* 'Elegantissima' behind it, not only for its own handsome cream-variegated leaves, cool and elegant under the pear blossom, but also to act as host for the clematis, which, out of season, has all the allure of Bognor in winter. On a support any colour will shine out. On the cornus, a blue or purple variety will show up best. 'Countess of Lovelace' is violet blue, 'Lasurstern' deep purple blue. 'Edouard Desfosse' is violet blue with a darker blue stripe down the centre of the petals, and conspicuous purple anthers.

1 *Pyrus* (Pear)

DECIDUOUS TREE
HEIGHT AND SPREAD
ACCORDING TO VARIETY
ZONE 5–9

There are several advantages in using a pear as the centrepiece of a planting scheme. First, of course, there is the delight of eating varieties of fruit that never find their way on to supermarket shelves; second is the pear's useful habit of growing naturally more upright than other fruit trees. 'Marguerite Marillat', a remarkably up-

right, neat tree, has fruit that is ready in September. Plant between November and March. Standards and half-standards require very little pruning, trained trees a great deal.

2 *Cornus alba* 'Elegantissima' (Dogwood)

DECIDUOUS SHRUB
HEIGHT AND SPREAD
8 x 8 FT/2.4 x 2.4 M
ZONE 3–8

This variegated dogwood has leaves broadly edged with white. The stems are reddish, though the bark is not as brilliant as a plain green variety such as 'Westonbirt'. It is a useful, undemanding shrub, which will spread to make a thicket of stems. It is fully hardy and will grow on a wide variety of soils, acid or alkaline, waterlogged or dry. Use in full sun or medium shade. In deep shade the growth will be lax. Cut back hard in early spring to encourage new growth which will have larger leaves and brighter bark than that on the old branches. Propagate by hardwood cuttings taken in October and November

3 *Cytisus x praecox* (Warminster broom)
DECIDUOUS SHRUB
HEIGHT AND SPREAD
5 X 5 FT/1.5 X 1.5 M
ZONE 6–9

Brooms are all stem and no leaf, which gives them a sparse appearance when they are out of flower. The pale creamy-yellow flowers smother the stems, which bend over in a graceful way under the burden. Each flower is like a tiny sweet pea. Brooms are best on light well-drained soil and they must have full sun. They do not like being moved. Do it at your peril. Plant in early autumn or late spring, but do not feed. This broom needs no regular pruning. Increase by taking cuttings with a heel in August or September. They are slow to root.

4 *Tulip*
BULB
HEIGHT AND SPREAD
ACCORDING TO VARIETY
ZONE 5–9

Tulips are the most beguiling of May bulbs, though not the longest-lived. Bulbs should not be planted before November as new growth induced by early planting may be subject to frost : Lord Mayor's Day is the traditional time. A sprinkling of bonemeal in each hole will help them on their way. A dibber is not the best tool to use for making holes : they arc gcncrally not big cnough for thc tulip to sit in comfortably and the

pointed end of the dibber often leaves a gap under the bulb where earth should be.

Use a trowel and excavate a decent home for the bulb if you want it to do its best. They thrive in alkaline soils. Add lime to heavy acid ground before planting. Dead-head the flowers when the petals fall, but leave the stem and foliage to feed the bulb below.

5 *Clematis* (Spring flowering)
DECIDUOUS CLIMBER
HEIGHT AND SPREAD
ACCORDING TO VARIETY
ZONE 5–9

The archetypal May clematis is, of course, *C. montana,* but it is extremely vigorous and will prove difficult to manage in a mixed planting. Give it a garage to play with. *C. macropetala* is more biddable, stopping at about 12 ft/3.6m. It has very pretty nodding semi-double flowers, deep blue in 'Maidwell Hall', 'Markham's Pink' as you would expect, pink. 'Snowbird' is a recent variety with whitc flowcrs and palc foliagc. It is later than others of its kind. All clematis do best with their feet in the shade and their heads in the sun. If you are planting on a trellis pyramid, set the roots on the north side of it and mulch well each spring, both to feed the roots and to insulate them. Clematis that flower in the early part of the year need no regular pruning. The simplest method of propagating is by layering in winter. Sever the layer when it has rooted.

In front of the pear, try a broom, perhaps *Cytisus x praecox* with a height and spread of about 5ft/1.5m. It is a graceful weeping shape and the flowers are a clean, soft yellow. It needs full sun. The trick with this group is not to clutter the ground too much. The rational explanation for this is that you do not want to starve the pear tree and so prevent it dropping luscious fruit into the trough in autumn. The irrational reason, far more important, is that you want in May to keep the maximum amount of space possible available for tulips. There may be one or two people in the world who choose not to grow tulips in their gardens, but such an aberration is scarcely to be credited. Think of green and white Viridiflora tulips with purple drumstick primulas, cream tulips with the bronze foliage of fennel, fat pink and white double tulips with blue cowichan primulas, lily-flowered china-pink tulips underplanted with a silver-leaved dead nettle, bright red tulips with mounds of lime-coloured *Euphorbia polychroma*, purple-black tulips such as 'Queen of Night' carpeted with the spiky silver foliage of dianthus. Kaufmanniana, Greigii, Fosteriana and single early types will all be too early for this May scheme. Choose instead from double earlies, mid-season, Darwin hybrids, Cottage, Parrot, Lily-flowered and Viridifloras. Heaven knows, it's enough. You will have arrived at the correct state of equilibrium when you spend more time choosing tulips than you do choosing clothes. The single group of the Viridifloras, so called because they all have some green in their petals, will provide some stunning tulips to complement the pale blossom of the pear tree. 'Spring Green' has very fresh green petals, each with a broad white edge, and grows to about 15in/38cm. 'Greenland' will warm the scheme up with a hint of pink in the elegant green-flushed flowers. The Parrots are madder, particularly 'Estella Rijnveld' which is a combination of rich raspberry-red and white, the whole flower crimped and waved in the most extraordinary manner.

Any duffers in the tulip family are outweighed by delights. 'Abu Hassan' is a memorable winner from the Triumph family, a deep, glossy mahogany with a yellow trim to the petals, mysterious with pale fruit blossom hovering over it. Colour photographs rarely do justice to the complexity or texture of tulip petals. Looking at pictures may be a doubtful way to choose tulips, but wading through salesmen's breathless prose is no easier. In the end, you must either take note of varieties you like in other people's gardens, or gamble on interpreting the no-man's-land between picture and prose. It will also be a gamble whether you get any flowers after the first, totally beguiling season. If you are too hard pressed to go through the rigmarole of lifting, trenching, drying and sorting tulip bulbs, leave them in the ground and persuade yourself that they are only annuals : it is wonderful what notions you can implant in the mind if you want to. Then, if your tulips flower again, you can look upon it as a bonus. If they do not, you do not hold it against them and there will be an opportunity to try out some different ones.

Some interesting work has been going on with tulips in recent years. Researchers have found that planting bulbs at twice the usual depth – at 8–10ins/20–25cm deep – decreases the tulip's propensity to break up into small bulblets after flowering. It is this exploding trick that normally stops the tulip from flowering the following season. Some types seem to be better repeat-flowerers than others. The yellow Fosteriana 'Candela' will do several seasons on the trot while 'Abu Hassan' is not a great stayer.

Luxuriance in the shade

Tulips, the broom and the pear will all do best in an open, sunny situation. The second scheme for May is made up of plants that will all grow happily in shade, provided it is the rich, moist sort of shade rather than the starved, dry kind. *Rubus x tridel* 'Benenden', an unprickly member of the blackberry family with large white papery flowers, provides the framework for a cool scheme of white, blue, pink and purple provided by an underplanting of herbaceous perennials. Although this scheme is designed with shade in mind, all the plants will be equally happy in sun, provided again that the soil is not dry or hungry. No one could pretend that *Rubus x tridel* 'Benenden', the centrepiece of this shady May plant group, is a tidy grower, so if you get fidgety when plants step out of line substitute the blameless choisya instead. If you are short of evergreens in the garden, the choisya may anyway be a better choice. It has handsome hand-shaped foliage of a bright glossy green and clusters of sweet-smelling white flowers that start towards the end of May and drift on through June and some of July. If you like speedy plants, stick with the rubus, for what it lacks in tidiness, it makes up for in growth. Its canes zoom up to 6ft/1.8m in a season and then arch over with the weight of the subsequent side shoots. It can spread over about 10ft/3m, but not in a bossy way. New stems are thrown up from the base each year. It is both wild and elegant, rather an unusual combination, and although it does nothing spectacular in the way of fruits or autumn colour, it is stunning in May when the white flowers come out all along the branches. In winter it is without interest. That will please the pessimists.

As it is such a loose grower, there is plenty of room under its wide spreading stems for a collection of other plants. In this way, it is more accommodating than the choisya, which sits dumpily and comfily down on the ground. Brunnera is an ideal companion for the rubus and provides between April and June (with some absent-minded extras through the rest of the year) a long succession of flowers like overgrown forget-me-nots,

1 *Rubus x tridel* 'Benenden'

DECIDUOUS SHRUB
HEIGHT AND SPREAD
8 X 10FT/2.4 X 3M
ZONE 5–9

This is a fast-growing ornamental member of the blackberry family that bears no fruit, but has large flat flowers of glistening white, displayed all along its branches in May. Each flower is 2in/5cm across and has a central boss of gold stamens. Plant between autumn and spring in any reasonable soil in sun or half shade, and mulch each spring with compost or rotted manure. After flowering each year, remove some of the old stems at ground level to encourage fresh growth. Propagate by layering in spring.

2 *Brunnera macrophylla*

DECIDUOUS PERENNIAL
HEIGHT AND SPREAD
18 X 24IN/45 X 60CM
ZONE 4–9

A hearty plant, verging on the coarse, but very generous with its sprays of forget-me-not-blue flowers. The leaves are ruthlessly efficient smotherers of weeds and, sadly, of anything else less robust that comes within their flopping range. Plant them in autumn or spring in any reasonable garden soil in sun or shade. They are far too robust to succumb to disease, but will appreciate a feed of mushroom compost or something similar each spring. Propagate by division in early spring.

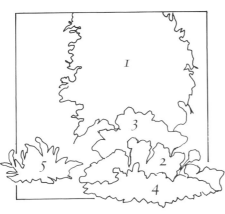

3 Astrantia (Masterwort)

DECIDUOUS PERENNIAL
HEIGHT AND SPREAD
24 X 24 IN/60 X 60 CM
ZONE 4–9

The variegated form of this, *A. major* 'Sunningdale Variegated', is a handsome foliage plant with five-lobed leaves, heavily splashed with cream. It thrives in shade and throws up heads of densely packed papery flowers, the general impression a greenish white. It should not be fed

too liberally or it may revert to plain green. Do not try and grow it in dry shade ; it will quickly droop. Shear the leaves to the ground in autumn, as the plant begins to look shabby. Divide established clumps in late spring.

4 Viola labradorica 'Purpurea'

SEMI-EVERGREEN PERENNIAL
HEIGHT AND SPREAD
4 X 12 IN/10 X 30 CM
ZONE 3–9

Leaves as well as flowers are purple, the leaves much the darker of the two. They are at their best in late spring. By the end of summer the purple has changed to dark green. This is an invaluable little plant for ground cover in shade, low growing and well-behaved. Unlike pansies, which thrive in full sun, the smaller violas appreciate dappled shade and a cool, deep, moist soil to get their roots into. This one does not flower so profligately as others of the family, but you should not skimp on watering or mulching. Dead-heading is also important in prolonging the display. This viola seeds itself about very freely, so you will be relieved of the task of propagating. It looks particularly good when it tucks itself into cracks in paving. Take care that it does not get swamped by the more ebullient members of this group. It may need help in this.

5 Convallaria
(Lily of the valley)

DECIDUOUS PERENNIAL
HEIGHT AND SPREAD
6 X 24 IN/15 X 60 CM
ZONE 4–8

This old favourite grows from a branched, creeping horizontal rhizome. It hates being disturbed and is slow to settle when newly planted. Where it is suited, that is, where there is cool, rich, damp soil, it spreads rapidly. The fresh green leaves are

quite strong enough to keep out weeds. 'Fortin's Giant' is a variety with larger flowers than the type. It has fatter bells, broader foliage and the useful tendency to flower a week or ten days later than the ordinary species. Plant both for a long succession of bloom. Plant the crowns in September or October just below the surface of soil that you have enriched with leaf-mould or compost. Top-dress each autumn when the leaves have died down with fresh food. Divide any time between October and March.

but without the mildew. The leaves, heart-shaped, are mid-green and a manageable size at this time of the year. Later they become coarse and will smother less robust neighbours. A clump will spread over about 2ft/60cm. Coming as it does from Siberia, it is completely hardy and absolutely trouble-free. Next to it, try one of the comfreys, perhaps a variety of *Symphytum grandiflorum,* which is equally thuggish in its attitude to neighbours. Comfrey is not a plant that deserves a starring role, less good than brunnera, but it is a useful filler with hairy pointed leaves and small clusters of tubular flowers in cream, pink and purple, depending on the variety. *S. grandiflorum* grows about 12in/30cm high. If you need a taller variety, look for *S. x uplandicum* with flowers in bluish-purple.

Away from this thugs' corner, make a separate group of variegated astrantia and polemonium. Three of each will make a clump that the eye will remember. Look for *Astrantia major* 'Sunningdale Variegated'. Its leaves are marked with creamy white. Flowers are crisp and papery, each one looking like a formal posy, in colour a rather washed-out pink, but they will not appear until later. In May it is the bold clumps of foliage that will provide interest. The polemonium, or Jacob's ladder, will give you flowers, masses of them, in purple spikes above mounds of finely cut, ferny foliage. It will flower more freely in the open, so if there are any shafts of sunlight in your shady patch, give them to this plant. The plants are not long-lived, but *P. caeruleum* is an enthusiastic self-seeder.

Round and about these groups, use lily of the valley and the purple-leaved *Viola labradorica purpurea.* For a splash of real colour add groups of the wild gladiolus *G. byzantinus,* if you are not intending to use it in June. It has flowers of an uncompromising magenta. The lily of the valley may try a takeover bid if it is suited, but it is not difficult to keep under control. There is a pink variety about, but the white is as sharp as malachite. The spears of leaves are a brilliant, fresh green and each one wraps round the flower like a florist's paper. The viola will need to be towards the front of your patch as it is only 6in/15cm high and could easily be smothered by the more brutish comfrey. The flowers, pale violet, are held well above the dark leaves.

Many superb plants have not yet got even a mention in these planting schemes for May. The month is profligate with possibilities. Some plants such as wisteria are far too aristocratic to mingle in mixed company. Wisteria, like a classic grand duchess, needs nothing but a support and a hundred years or so behind it. It is particularly brilliant hanging down over a pergola, but you must arrange the height carefully so that as you stroll through underneath, the blooms merely brush the top of your head rather than swinging damply into your face. Its mere presence lends an air of elegance to any garden.

The trunk quickly achieves that twisted, venerable form that the Chinese write poems about. But, as we have said, it is not a great mixer.

Ferns are also at their best this month, but their elegance is even more understated than the wisteria's. Ferns creep up on you slowly and are likely to hit you between the eyes only when you have been gardening for half a dozen years or so. As new gardeners, colour is what thrills us most, but as we get drawn deeper into the whole business, we find ourselves admiring more and more those plants that have fine form. In ferns, this is paramount. Their beauty in May will be more apparent if you remember in spring to cut away the old foliage that has weathered the winter. Then the primeval young shoots, furled like bishops' crosiers, untrammelled by garbage, can make their full effect. They need space about them if the form is to be as well balanced as nature intended and in mixed plantings are best used with plants that snuffle around at ground level and so will not get in the ferns' way. Then the fronds can erupt and fan out with the symmetry that is built into every fern's soul. Even the mad ferns, the ones with beards on the ends of their fronds or bunches of parsley attached to each pair of pinnae, are symmetrically dotty. The larger part of the group would choose soils that are just the acid side of neutral and positions that are moist and shaded. The lively family of harts' tongues (*Phyllitis scolopendrium*), however, thrive in lime soils and many of the others will grow in neutral soils, provided that they are neither baked nor starved. If you look at the places ferns put themselves in the wild this gives useful pointers to the ways in which we can use their hybrid cousins in the garden.

Small ferns, such as spleenworts, that you are unlikely to trip over can usefully be tucked into the risers of steps, brick, concrete or stone. Evergreen – or more truthfully winter-green – kinds such as the harts' tongues can tick over gently in the gloomiest sub-basement yard during the months of November to February when so much else has dived underground for cover. The harts' tongue is unusual among British native ferns as it is not divided, but boldly strap-shaped with fronds anything up to 30in/75cm long, rich glossy green. Like the rest of the fern family, it has erupted into some bizarre forms. *Phyllitis scolopendrium ramo-cristata* has fronds which branch repeatedly and end in flat frilled crests. *P. s. undulata* has broad fronds with wavy, crimped margins. The names are a mouthful. As each new form emerges (and ferns, having slippery genes, delight in bobbing up in different disguises) botanists bolt yet another suffix on to the standard tag, rather as Germans build up their marathon portmanteau words. You must pray you are never called upon to ask for a fern by name, but can point dumbly instead.

One of the most elegant of the hardy ferns is the ostrich fern, *Matteuccia struthiopteris*, not a native but eager to naturalize where it is happy. In the wild it grows in moist peaty woodland places and it will be hopeless expecting it to do its astonishing erupting trick out of a sun-baked urn, however ravishing you think the effect may be. In form it is one of the most beautiful of all the ferns, a compact upright shuttlecock shape as the fronds first emerge, spreading into a wider whorl as they expand through the summer. Think of it in a shady moist corner, or rather, think of them, for three will look better than one, carpeted perhaps with a spread of blue forget-me-nots, or with a small variegated periwinkle creeping round their feet. Nothing too distracting should be used with them. In their haughty, take-it-or-leave-it way ferns need to dominate their space.

Geometric patterns

While you are waiting for ferns to creep up on you (and – if you stay with gardening – they will) here is a rather less restrained planting scheme for May, which will suit a formal box-edged bed, part of a small parterre or some small geometric shape that can be divided into regular portions. If you have a small square bed, trace out a diamond within it, the corners of the diamond touching the centre points of the edges of the square. This will leave you with five distinct planting areas. A circular bed can be divided up into a series of ever-decreasing concentric circles, a Pooteresque arrangement that is entirely in keeping with the frontage of a Victorian terraced house.

Returning to blossom, the central theme of a May garden, think of planting a standard tree in the centre of your geometric plot. This could be a small, elegant crab apple such as *Malus sargentii* which grows no more than 6–8ft/1.8–2.4m high, but spreads rather wider. In mid-May pink-tinted buds open to masses of fresh white blossom followed by glossy leaves. The autumn fruit is bright red, the size of cherries. It could be a standard hawthorn which, though a wildling, adapts with alacrity to the high life. The true wild species is *Crataegus monogyna* but for garden purposes *C. x lavallei* may be a better choice. It makes a smaller, denser tree than the hedgerow species and has large glossy dark green leaves that often hang on until Christmas, making a splendid backdrop for the big orange berries. The late-May blossom is white and profuse. The formal effect will be heightened if you clip the hawthorn into a regular rounded shape, balanced on its long straight trunk.

The tree will be a permanent anchor to what, each year, can be a changing series of patterns round its feet. Three, or at the most four, different plants together will be plenty. The old-fashioned double daisies, *Bellis perennis,* are ideal to use in this sort of scheme, perhaps the variety 'Pomponette Rose' contrasted with blue puschkinia (low pale blue bell flowers, closely related to the scillas), or white daisies with yellow violas, partnered by some of the dainty Poeticus narcissi, either 'Actaea' or the later-flowering Pheasant's Eye. All the violas are excellent for this sort of scheme, as, with a little attention to dead-heading, they have a long season of flowering. Try forget-me-nots together with the rich, velvety, almost black flowers of the viola 'Molly Sanderson'. Add if you like a contrasting variety such as the pale lemon 'Moonlight' or 'Little David'. Underplant the crab with blocks of blue viola ('Boughton Blue' is an excellent, vigorous type) and contrasting blocks of the small variegated periwinkle *Vinca minor* 'Argenteo-variegata' with leaves boldly splashed with cream. The periwinkle will not get going as fast as you think it should, but like a player in the game of grandmother's footsteps, it does best when you are not watching it. The advantages of using a plant such as vinca with evergreen foliage are obvious. The patch that it grows in will look furnished and comfortable for the whole of the rest of the year and you could give it fresh companions for each May display.

London pride (*Saxifraga x urbium*), underrated because it is so common, is another excellent neat foliage plant that can be pressed into service for a geometric May display. In May, of course, it is in flower – spidery wiry stems about 12in/30cm high, topped with ethereal pale pink stars – but its chunky, succulent foliage is a year-long delight. It never seems to have an off season, even in February when everything, including the gardener, is feeling distinctly *à bout de forces*. It has a cousin, a cross between saxifrage and geum, *S. x geum* 'Dentata', that is even more desirable, for each of its spoon-shaped evergreen leaves has a neat zigzag edge, as if it had been cut round with pinking shears. This, used with a small aquilegia – perhaps the startlingly blue *Aquilegia alpina* – would make an equally good ingredient to use in a formal May bed.

1 *Malus sargentii* (Crab apple)

DECIDUOUS TREE
HEIGHT AND SPREAD
8 X 10FT/2.4 X 3M
ZONE 4–9

Crabs grow equally well in full sun or light shade. The only thing that will set them back is heavy, water-logged soil. Dig in plenty of humus before you plant. Standards or half-standards are more formal than bush shapes and allow you plenty of room for underplanting. Plant in autumn or spring and mulch in early spring. No regular pruning is required, but dead or straggly shoots can be cut out in February. Species such as *M. sargentii* will come true from seed sown in autumn, but take up to ten years to reach flowering size.

In confined spaces this is a useful tree, reaching only one third the size of most crab apples. The flowers are glistening white with greenish centres. They are massed in clusters on the branches. The fruits are bright red, in some autumns making a dramatic contrast with the yellow-tinted foliage. The crabs are a well-endowed family with excellent blossom in white or pink, showy fruits and in some cases, autumn colour too.

2 *Bellis perennis* (Double daisy)

PERENNIAL, GROWN AS
BIENNIAL
HEIGHT AND SPREAD
6 X 9 IN/15 X 22 CM
ZONE 6–9

The easiest way to acquire quantities of these is to grow them yourself. Scatter the seed in a shallow drill outside in June, transplant or thin out the seedlings when they are large enough to handle and set them in their final positions in September or October. The plants will do best in

rich, moist soil. Keep an eye out for slugs. Regular dead-heading will prolong the display of flowers and prevent too much self-seeding: seed strains often degenerate until self-sown plants are no different from the daisies that grow in the lawn. The 'Pomponette' series is an excellent dwarf strain and 'White Carpet' a uniform, compact variety. 'Radar Red' has bigger flowers in a show-stopping colour. 'Goliath' has the biggest flowers.

3 *Vinca minor* 'Variegata' (Periwinkle)

EVERGREEN SUB-SHRUB
HEIGHT AND SPREAD
4 X 24 IN/10 X 60 CM
ZONE 7–10

The Romans used the wiry stems of periwinkle to bind into wreaths. They are very tough. *V. minor* is a neater, less invasive version of the common periwinkle, which in small gardens can appear coarse. It takes its time in covering the ground and will need a certain amount of hand weeding until it becomes established. The narrow leaves are brightly variegated and flowers can be blue, white or plum-coloured. Mulching with crushed bark after planting will help keep down weeds. They are good in shade but the creamy variegation will be brighter in good light. They can easily be clipped back if they over-reach their boundaries. The plant propagates itself as it grows for the trailing stems root from every node where they touch the soil. You can encourage it by sifting fine compost on top of the long stems.

4 *Viola*

SEMI-EVERGREEN PERENNIAL
HEIGHT AND SPREAD
4 X 12 IN/10 X 30 CM
ZONE 3–9

These are profligate flowers but to keep up this superhuman display, they need feeding. Dead-heading is also important in prolonging the display. If plants get leggy, cut stems back to a joint close to the base of the plant. Established plants should be sheared back in autumn. Propagate by sowing seed in July and August or take cuttings of basal shoots in July.

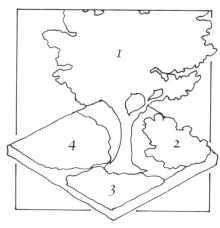

JUNE

A JUNE GARDEN SHOULD BE SWOONING WITH MORE SCENTS THAN A seraglio : roses, of course, honeysuckle, viburnum, untidy sprays of sweet rocket, philadelphus and the sharp, acrid smell of catmint. It is much easier to describe the way a plant looks than how it smells. English is a rich language, but words to convey smell usually leave one floundering in a bog of overwriting. You can describe one smell in terms of another and say perhaps that a certain flower smells of cowslips, but to the increasing hordes of people who have never clapped eyes – even less their noses – to a cowslip, this will be unhelpful. Although flower smells themselves are extremely sensuous, the words to describe them are terse : sweet, heavy, spicy. 'Sweet' is the most over-used description of all. There is a world of difference between the light but rich sweetness of mock orange (*Philadelphus coronarius*) and the heavy, almost overpowering sweetness of the climbing *Hydrangea petiolaris*. Scent is rarely mentioned as one of this plant's attributes, but it is incredibly strong this month, all the power coming from the tiny nondescript flowers in the centre of each corymb, not from the large surrounding florets. The busy Victorians, who were keen on sorting and classifying, made an attempt to identify flower perfumes according to the chemical substance that predominated in each essential oil. The resulting groups – indoloid, aminoid, and benzoloid – unfortunately sound more like the products of a motorway service station than the heady perfumes of the flower garden.

Another problem with smells is holding them clearly in the mind. A dog seems able to do this with consummate ease. Even the least intelligent hound can pick up a good deal of information through its nose and, to them, a sniff round a trouser leg seems a surer guide to identification than a once-over with the eyes. If you close your eyes and think of a philadelphus, it is quite easy to remember what the shrub looks like. You can recall the shape of its leaf and flower, the general outline and the relative size of the shrub in its entirety. Its precise smell is not so easy to conjure up. You remember that it is supposed to smell like orange blossom, but what does that smell like ? It is odd that a smell should be so elusive, for it is among the most emotive of the senses. One sniff of a sweet pea can open up a whole Pandora's box of emotions : rows, reconciliations, a particular meal, a birthday party. A garden without smells would be a hamstrung thing. You should certainly have plenty of scented plants in the garden in June, when there is the happy possibility of lying on the grass, letting the different smells drift over you like a mute nocturne. There is also the possibility that you will instead smell the paraffin and burnt steak of your neighbour's barbecue.

Scented climbers are a boon, particularly when placed so that scent can drift in the evening through open windows and doors. The large-flowered clematis resolutely refuse to oblige. There is a double white, 'Duchess of Edinburgh', which received an FCC, a First Class Certificate, from the Royal Horticultural Society in 1876. It was described then as 'very sweet scented', but even the most questing, expensively insured nose will be hard put to it to find any scent there now. Gerard, Parkinson and other early horticulturists all mention white jasmine, *Jasminum officinale*, as being the best of all scented climbers, perfect to frame the arbour where you could toss off a quick sonnet between your labours. The leaf is rich and healthy and, in most places, evergreen. Modern writers plump for honeysuckle. Some types are more strongly scented than others and all rev up more in the evening than during the day. This is not so much to delight the June gardener as to attract moths, on which honeysuckles depend for pollination. They are the only insects with tongues long enough to reach down the honeysuckle's tube to the nectar at the bottom. During the day, when the moths are not flying, there is no need to turn on the come-hither smell.

With the flaming exception of red roses, many of the most heavily scented flowers are white : mock orange, the summer jasmine, madonna lilies, gardenia, late spring's lily of the valley. It seems as if the smell has intensified to make up for the lack of colour. Blue flowers, apart from the spicily scented bluebell, have least smell. Think of ceanothus, delphinium, forget-me-not, campanula. For the most part, blue flowers are pollinated by bees. Bees, like us, work by sight rather than smell.

Why anybody ever buys a rose without a scent is a mystery. As a rule, the old roses have the edge over the modern ones, for piquancy and variety of fragrance, but even among the Hybrid Teas, there are some that are markedly more smelly than others. Deep cerise pink 'Wendy Cussons' is an awkward grower, but smells richly of damask. The velvety crimson 'Ena Harkness' is another good HT rose with as much delight for the nose as for the eye.

'Constance Spry' looks like an old rose, but is a modern shrub or climber. It has huge cabbagy double pink flowers that carry a spicy smell. The Damask rose 'Ispahan' is equally overpowering with small, tightly packed flowers of a slightly deeper shade of pink. 'Yellow Wings', a modern shrub rose, has a lighter, more fleeting smell than either the Damasks or the Hybrid Musks, but this is perfectly in keeping with its huge floppy single yellow flowers. The Hybrid Musks 'Penelope' and 'Buff Beauty' are both worth more than an absent-minded sniff and the Alba 'Celeste' is the best of all. For their scent as well as for the colour and beauty of their flowers, roses have an indispensable place in a June garden. Unfortunately, undressed, few of them have bodies to boast about.

Many rose bushes are gawky, gaunt and an embarrassment to the eye when they are not in flower. In mixed plantings, it is important therefore to use roses with plants that do have good form and foliage and which can carry the rose when its brief season is over. There are some roses which themselves have good leaves. The Rugosa family has bright, fresh foliage, blessedly free from black spot and mildew (but not from rust), the leaves deeply corrugated. *R. glauca* has handsome pewter-coloured foliage, an excellent foil for the pale briar-like flowers. Apart from these stalwarts, leaves are not a rose's great strength. In the matter of general form, the old roses have the edge over modern Hybrid Teas. They are not always tidy, but they put themselves about gracefully with longer, laxer growth than that of the Hybrid Teas. It is odd that the old roses' habit of flowering only once in a season should so virulently be held against them. Nobody expects lilac, or philadelphus or hydrangea to put on a 'We never close' show and the fact that lilac is an ugly grower with undistinguished foliage has never stopped it being planted for its one brief, but swoony flowering in May. Dissatisfaction with the one-off roses probably crept in when the Hybrid Perpetuals were introduced in the middle of the nineteenth century. This was followed by the success of the repeat-flowering Hybrid Teas which had 'Never mind the quality, feel the colour' stamped all over them.

A good rose should be beautiful in more than bloom. It should grow with grace and form into a bush that is not a pain to look at for ten months of the year. Its foliage should be decent enough not to detract from the overall effect. It should have a rich smell. Individual flowers should have beauty of form as well as of colour. A good rose will have a healthy constitution and not be a martyr to mildew and black spot. There may be bonuses such as autumn leaf colour (*R. virginiana* is particularly good in this respect) or good hips. No rose is perfect, but in mixed plantings certainly, the old type of shrubby rose is easier to use than the Hybrid Teas. The Rugosa 'Blanche Double de Coubert' comes as close to perfection as any. The flowers are half double, of a pure, chalky white, although the buds have a cream tinge. The smell is magnificent and after a great flush of bloom in June, it produces odd flowers throughout the rest of the summer. It makes a big bush, at least 5ft/1.5m high, and as much wide, with bright green crinkly leaves, extremely effective as a background for the dead-white flowers. Its only fault is that flowers get browned by rain. It was introduced in 1892, one of the large family of Rugosa roses, which all have excellent foliage and large, rather floppy, open flowers, all beautifully scented. The turn of the century was a good time for Rugosas. The lovely wine-purple 'Roseraie de l'Hay' was introduced in 1901 and also 'Fru Dagmar Hastrup', a papery, single pink rose which has brilliant round hips in the autumn. All the Rugosas make sturdy bushes and need little pruning. You only need to cut out dead wood in spring, together with any excessively thin and twiggy growths.

The Hybrid Musks are technically modern shrub roses, though made very much in the old style. Most of them were bred by a horticultural vicar of the 1920s, the Rev. Joseph Pemberton of Essex. He bequeathed his stock to his gardeners, John and Ann Bentall, and they subsequently produced 'Buff Beauty', one of the best of the group, with closely packed clusters of buff-yellow flowers, tinged with apricot. Flowering starts in mid-June, but there is a useful second flush later in the season. 'Buff Beauty' opens from tight little buds of rich apricot flushed with red into clusters of flowers which fade as they open to various shades of clotted cream. The stems are not as strong as they might be and this is a weakness you notice particularly after rain, a depressingly regular aspect of the June scene.

Ramblers grown up tripods also make a fine centrepiece for a June planting, though will look naked through the winter. Gertrude Jekyll often used 'The Garland' in this way. It has flexible, easily trained stems and wide clusters of small, pink-flushed flowers which smell of oranges. Avoid monsters like 'Kiftsgate' in this position : you will never be able to keep on top of it, though it is wonderful where it can be given its head, to clothe an arbour or drape itself about in a big tree. The Multiflora rambler 'Goldfinch' would be suitable as the centrepiece for a scheme in yellow. It has tightly packed clusters of small, cupped, semi-double flowers, golden-yellow fading to cream. The foliage is clean, lush and glossy and the stems almost thornless. It stops at about 8ft/2.4m. It flowers in a single flush. 'New Dawn', introduced in 1930, continues throughout the summer and in a mild winter will even produce a slightly moth-eaten flower for a Christmas posy. Fat buds open to semi-double flowers of soft pink, usually held in clusters. The foliage is plentiful, but not as glossy as 'Goldfinch'. Both are tolerant of some shade. The Chinensis climber 'Phyllis Bide' is more complicated in colouring, yellow, cream, pink and orange all drifting into each other, the colours deepening as the flowers age. It grows vigorously with plenty of twiggy side shoots and has two flushes of bloom during the summer. The Japanese, the most refined gardeners in the world, rather despise roses and consider them crude efforts of nature. It would be contrary to make an English garden without a single rose in it, but there is room for only a few in the following planting schemes for June. Choose cool schemes of white and mauve and blue, beefed up with slashes of magenta and acid green.

The old Bourbon rose 'Boule de Neige' can adapt itself easily to mixed plantings. It grows about 4ft/1.2m high, with a spread of slightly less. It is upright in habit, which leaves the ground below free for you to tinker around with violas or catmint or what you will, and is repeat-flowering, a bonus with the old roses. It has dark green leaves and fully double globular flowers, pure white and smelling of paradise. French names always add a touch of sumptuousness to a rose. 'Snowball' sounds banal ; 'Boule de Neige' is magnificent. The Portland rose 'Comte de Chambord' is another outstanding rose for mixed plantings, more compact than the Bourbon and more or less continuous in its flower throughout the summer. These are large, considering the size of the bush, packed with rich pink petals, more extravagantly ruffled than a 'Come Dancing' dress and richly scented. The Albas are an exceptionally healthy gang of roses and of very ancient lineage. *R. alba* 'Maxima' has been around since the fifteenth century and has double white flowers. 'Celeste' is semi-double with soft pink flowers. They both look terrific with catmint, purple petunias or *Verbena bonariensis*. They make big bushes, about 6ft/1.8m high, by 4ft/1.2m wide, but do not start to flower until late June, continuing through July. The scent will knock you sideways.

Scents of the seraglio

A philadelphus (mock orange) and a Hybrid Musk rose provide the anchors for this first planting scheme in white, buff, pale blue and magenta with buffers of green-flowering alchemilla. As with some other shrubs, such as rose and honeysuckle, there has been a lunatic trend among the breeders of philadelphus to go for flower size at the expense of smell. There is little point in growing a philadelphus that does not knock you out with its scent, so avoid varieties such as 'Boule d'Argent' and 'Dame Blanche'. If you are short of space, use one of the upright-growing varieties such as 'Virginal' with double white scented flowers – and a lot of them. 'Avalanche' is also an upright grower with masses of scented flowers. If you have room for a bush that is as wide as it is tall, choose 'Belle Etoile' with single white flowers, stained purple in the centre. Whatever variety you choose, after the first three years of doing nothing, you should cut out some of the old flowered stems in July each year. If, as most gardeners do, you are trying to cram a quart into a pint pot, abandon the philadelphus and build round the rose. If you use the philadelphus, disguise the undistinguished foliage by running a clematis through it, preferably one that will come into flower when the philadelphus is over. A magenta-tinted variety such as 'Ernest Markham' would blend well with this particular scheme. Pearly white 'Huldine' would echo the mock orange's own flowers through July and August. If you have chosen an upright philadelphus, there will be room to put a sprawling shrub rose in front of it. The Hybrid Musk rose 'Penelope' is lovely in such a situation, despite its faults, mentioned earlier, of lax growth and stems sometimes barely strong enough to hold up the double flowers. The colour is exactly what is needed here, however : creamy-buff. If the disadvantages of this rose seem to weigh heavier than the advantages, try perhaps 'Hebe's Lip', an old variety, reintroduced round about 1912. This is a bushy plant, also slightly inclined to sprawl, but you do not want another shrub shooting up like a rocket if you have chosen an upright philadelphus. 'Hebe's Lip', also known as 'Reine Blanche' has large, loose, semi-double flowers of cream, edged with pink. The foliage is grey-green, like the Albas, and is faintly scented. The whole bush is more compact than 'Penelope' but it has only one burst of flowers, whereas the Hybrid Musks absent-mindedly produce blooms throughout the summer.

Around and under the philadelphus and the rose, grow clouds of catmint, which is invaluable for a long summer display. Choice of variety will again depend on what space you have to spare. 'Six Hills Giant' is a superb plant, but two of them planted together will easily account for 6ft/1.8m of border. *Nepeta nervosa* is one of the smallest varieties, only about 12in/30cm high. They are good-tempered plants, easy to manage, with aromatic matt grey foliage and spikes of small, lipped flowers of a distinctly greyish blue. With the catmint, plant clumps of *Gladiolus byzantinus*, which has bright green sword-shaped leaves and brilliant magenta flowers. This is nowhere near a match for the bullies that Dame Edna Everage so dotes on. She would scarcely think it worth the name of gladdy, but it is an altogether easier thing to work into mixed plantings than the blockbusters that usually go by the name. It is fully hardy, the corms do not need to be lifted and dried and it grows no more than 2ft/60cm high. If any kind of gladioli brings on a fit of expletives, then go instead for mounds of the magenta-flowered *Geranium psilostemon*. Its general outline is similar to that of the catmint, however : the gladiolus takes up less space and its foliage, strong and upright, provides a better contrast with the mounds of catmint.

1 *Philadelphus* (Mock orange)

DECIDUOUS SHRUB
HEIGHT AND SPREAD
From 5 x 5 FT to 10 x 10 FT/1.5
x 1.5M to 3 x 3M
ZONE 5–9

Easy-going and therefore often neglected garden shrubs with clusters of fairly short-lived blossom in June or July. Flowers are cream or white, some with a purple blotch inherited from *P. coulteri*, parent of many modern hybrids. Some varieties have given up their scent for the sake of bigger flowers. It is a bad trade-off. 'Avalanche' has sweetly scented, pure white flowers and leaves that are smaller than average. Regular pruning keeps them up to scratch: do this as soon as the blossom is over, cutting out all the old flowered stems. If you have inherited an overgrown monster, cut half of it to the ground after it has flowered in midsummer and follow on with the other half the year after. After a year catching up, the rejuvenated growth will flower more freely than the old. They are tolerant of all soils and will grow happily in sun or half shade. Propagate by cuttings of half-ripe lateral shoots in July or August, or by hardwood cuttings taken in October or November.

2 *Rose* 'Penelope'

DECIDUOUS SHRUB
HEIGHT AND SPREAD
4 x 4 FT/1.2 x 3M
ZONE 6–9

In mixed plantings, use shrub roses rather than the more angular Hybrid Teas. Hybrid Musk roses are a particularly graceful and easy group, bred during the first quarter of this century by an enthusiastic vicar, the Rev. Joseph Pemberton. He was already 61 when he introduced his

first roses in 1913. 'Penelope' came on the scene in 1924 and is typical of this group of long-flowering, sweet-scented roses. There are two main flushes of flower in early and late summer with some odd blooms thrown into the gap between. As a family they are tolerant of poor soils and they also put up with semi-shaded positions. 'Penelope' is slightly susceptible to mildew. Use fungicides if necessary to keep it at bay. Regular pruning is not necessary, but if you do cut out old wood, new shoots will spring from the base. Growth is naturally fan-shaped, but you may find some of the lower stems get smothered by eager perennials. If so, prop them up discreetly.

J U N E · Scheme 1

Scents of the seraglio

3 *Nepeta* (Catmint)
DECIDUOUS PERENNIAL
HEIGHT AND SPREAD
30 X 30 IN/75 X 75 CM
ZONE 6–9

An invaluable clump-forming plant with grey-green aromatic foliage and sprays of grey-blue flowers. It grows quickly enough to smother annual weeds and being itself gently indeterminate in colour, fits in easily with border companions. Cut clumps back hard after the first flowering to encourage a repeat performance later in the summer. In cold areas, leave the withered stems for winter protection. It prefers full sun and well-drained soil. Increase by dividing in spring.

4 *Geranium psilostemon*
DECIDUOUS PERENNIAL
HEIGHT AND SPREAD
24 X 24 IN/60 X 60 CM
ZONE 4–8

Stunning magenta flowers with black centres shine out over mounds of elegantly cut foliage. This is a star among the endlessly useful tribe of geraniums, with a long season of flowering through June and July. The leaves are as much of an asset as the flowers, for they form sturdy, weed-smothering clumps. Later in autumn, when the flowers are over frosts sometimes turns the foliage rich red.

It thrives in any ordinary well-drained garden soil, in sun or part shade. In exposed situations, you may need to prop growth with short pea-sticks. Generally it needs no help. Cut back old stems to the ground when they have finished flowering. This often promotes a second flush of flowering in late summer. Divide the plants if necessary between September and March. If flower heads are not removed, the plants self-seed.

5 *Alchemilla mollis* (Lady's mantle)
DECIDUOUS PERENNIAL
HEIGHT AND SPREAD
20 X 20 IN/50 X 50 CM
ZONE 4–9

Useful ground-cover plant with scalloped leaves of a downy texture. Sprays of tiny greenish-yellow flowers are carried through the summer. Sometimes a late cold spell burns the edges of the leaves and stops them opening fully; cut these off. It is fully hardy and grows in any soil, in sun or shade. Cut back to the ground in autumn.

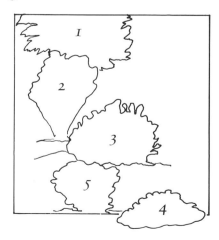

The rest is trimming. Annual eschscholzia, though impossible to pronounce (try Californian poppy instead) can now be got in wonderful mixtures of what the seed companies call 'art shades', shades of Oscar Wilde's aesthetes, the same buffs and creams and pinks that make the 'Penelope' rose such a winner. As its common name suggests, it likes full sun and a dry, sandy soil to flower most prolifically. It also needs some dead-heading. The seed pods are long and curved and the plant, if allowed to, will self-seed willingly. Not all gardeners look on this as an asset, which is churlish of them. Gradually over a few years, the flowers from these self-set plants drift back to the plain orange that they were before breeders took hold of them, with none of the creams and deep purples that make the mixtures so exciting. Like most plants with carroty roots, they do not transplant easily and seed is best sown in late spring, where you want the flowers. Germination is quite quick, between two or three weeks, and the seedlings, with their ferny sea-green foliage, are easy to distinguish from the usual weed seedlings – annual meadow grass, groundsel, speedwell – that will inevitably germinate with them. Sow the seed as thinly as you can and then you will not waste too many seedlings in the thinning process. 'Double Ballerina Mixed' is a good strain with wide silky flowers splaying open from tightly furled buds. Like drunks at a packed party, the flowers hold each other up by leaning on each other and will give a long display through until the end of September. If you still have space for more, introduce cool green pools of alchemilla, one of those plants that, like the best sort of aunt, gets along in any company. You can have too much of it and here it is probably sensible practice to shear off the flower heads before they start casting their seeds about.

Red, white and blue

The white Rugosa rose 'Blanche Double de Coubert' is the centrepiece of a second planting scheme for June, which introduces another of the month's stars, the peony. It wins no marks for length of flowering, but while the flowers are out, they are stunning enough to take the spotlight away from anything else in the garden. Deep reds and pinks are the kinds that are wanted for this scheme in white, deep red, silver and blue. Most of the cultivars around today are the children of the old European double red peony *P. officinalis*, still a favourite in cottage gardens, and the Chinese species *P. lactiflora*. Hybridization started in France in the 1820s and the breeders' names – Dessert, Crousse – are commemorated still in the flowers that they left behind. 'Felix Crousse' is a bright deep carmine-coloured double. 'Auguste Dessert' is a bright salmon rose double, with petals edged in silver. Foliage colours well in autumn. There are three things you need to know if you are to succeed with peonies. Sadly for the peonies, many people only know two. Most important is the fact that they must not be planted too deep. On heavy soils, 1in/2.5cm of earth on top of the crown is plenty. Even in light soils, twice that depth will be more than enough. Leaves may fight their way through, but if the plant is lodged suffocatingly deep, it will never flower. If you have a peony that is shy in this way, lift it in the autumn and replant it at a shallower level. The second rule has to do with the peony's temperament. It is an odd mixture of flash-in-the-pan and stayer. The flowers are dramatic, gaudy and short-lived, but the plant itself, once settled, lives an astonishingly long time. In the days BC (before conversion) when there were still half-ruined cottages in the countryside, you would sometimes see crimson flowers blazing away among tall grass. Usually it would turn out to be the old double red *P. officinalis* 'Rubra Plena', a cottage garden favourite since the seventeenth century. Although a peony may survive half a century of neglect, it cannot stand disturbance. Garden around it as carefully as if it were a piece of Ming porcelain. The third precept is not as vital as the other two, but makes all the difference between a decent plant and a dazzling one. Peonies appreciate good food, plenty of humus and rotted manure dug into the ground during the summer before they are planted and a liberal measure of bonemeal and mulch thereafter.

The flowers are named after Paeon, physician to the Greek gods. The old European variety, *P. officinalis*, introduced here by the Romans, was looked on as an elixir for all ills. It was said to cure jaundice, kidney pains and epilepsy, to prevent nightmares and lift depression. In the eighteenth century Hannah Glasse was still recommending peony roots for weak hearts and stomachs. It took off as a garden flower in the mid-nineteenth century and now there are at least 150 hybrids to choose from, as well as some elegant species. The common double crimson opens in May, most of the hybrids in June. Doubles last longer in flower than singles, but are more difficult to stake and keep the right way up if there is a rainstorm. There is a third type, which Kelways calls 'Imperials'; others call them anemone-flowered. They have strong, bowl-shaped outer petals like the singles, but the stamens have turned into thread-like petals, making a huge fluffy boss in the centre of each flower, sometimes the same colour as the outside petals, sometimes contrasting. 'Bowl of Beauty' is a good peony of this type, rich pink petals with a creamy white centre. Of the doubles, there is no end. Avoid taller varieties such as 'Arabian Prince' which will be difficult to tuck in under the branches of the rose. Look for a reasonably compact type such as 'France' which is 32in/78cm high, with rose-pink petals. Some varieties are more sweetly scented than others. 'Glory of

1 *Paeonia* (Peony)

DECIDUOUS PERENNIAL
HEIGHT AND SPREAD
3 X 3 FT/90 X 90 CM
ZONE 7—9

If they could choose, peonies would give themselves an open sunny spot in soil that is rich and slightly on the heavy side, but certainly not water-logged. If you have a light soil, take particular note of feeding and mulch like mad. They will not flower in deep shade, but can cope perfectly well

with a partially shaded site. Most mail order specialists, such as Kel-ways, send out their plants bare-rooted in autumn. Certainly they should be in the ground before Christmas. Make a good big hole when you are ready to plant and settle some good rich soil round the roots: manure here will lead to dire dis-eases. The plant will take sev-eral years to settle properly and may not flower at all in its first year. When it does get into its stride, it may need staking. Double varieties are, of course, more in-clined to flop than singles. Do any necessary buttressing in

spring before growth is too far ad-vanced. Push twiggy sticks into the ground around the peony, or use semi-circular iron supports. Water if the ground gets dry, and cut down the stems just below ground level when the foliage has died. Some var-ieties, such as the single maroon 'Sir Edward Elgar' and the double blush white 'Kelways Supreme', have good autumn foliage, so you should not be in too much of a hurry to tidy them up.

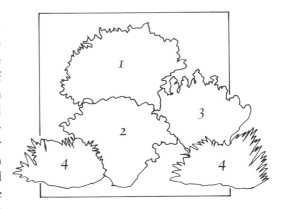

JUNE · Scheme 2
Red, white and blue

2 *Rosa rugosa* 'Blanc Double de Coubert'
DECIDUOUS SHRUB
HEIGHT AND SPREAD
5 x 4 FT/1.5 x 1.2 CM
ZONE 6–9

The rugosa roses are upright and bushy in growth and have remarkably good bright foliage, too rough to be a welcome resting place for black spot spores. 'Blanc Double de Coubert' is one of the most outstanding hybrids, raised in France in 1892. It has huge numbers of dead white, papery flowers opening from slightly creamy buds. Unfortunately they brown in the rain. It does not fruit as dramatically as single Rugosas such as 'Frau Dagmar Hastrup', but the foliage is a pleasant soft yellow in autumn. It makes a showy, dense bush. It will put up with less than ideal soils, though growth and vigour will be much improved by an annual mulch. No regular pruning is needed. Suckers must be taken out.

3 *Campanula* (Bellflower)
DECIDUOUS PERENNIAL
HEIGHT AND SPREAD
36 x 18 IN/90 x 45 CM
ZONE 4–9

The standard types of border campanulas, *C. latifolia*, *C. latiloba* and so on, are not fussy about soil, though in the wild, most are found on limy ground. They are also very tolerant of shade, though again, left to themselves, they would choose a spot which was in sun for at least part of the day. They enjoy being split and replanted in fresh ground every

couple of years. Some may try and put themselves in fresh ground without your help. They do not need lush feeding – they are used to fighting for survival – but a handful of bonemeal each spring will cheer them up considerably. They are wonderfully resilient to pest and disease. Increase stock by dividing in spring. Many members of this family make good companions for shrub roses. The blue tones have a hint of grey, which blends well with their dusky colours.

4 *Artemisia*
SEMI-EVERGREEN PERENNIAL
HEIGHT AND SPREAD
12 x 24 IN/30 x 60 CM
ZONE 5–9

This creeps slowly about to make soft hummocks of very finely cut silver foliage. 'Nana' is a particularly dwarf form (3 x 8in/7.5 x 20cm). Sun is its usual requirement, but it will grow in shade if it is not too dense. *A. stelleriana* will cope with deeper shade and damper soil than *A. schmidtiana*. It grows about 12in/30cm tall and has white felted leaves, cut like a chrysanthemum's so the effect is quite heavy. All artemisias prefer light soil. Dig in plenty of sand to improve drainage. Trim *A. schmidtiana* lightly in spring. Cut down stems of *A. stelleriana* in autumn. Propagate by dividing clumps in spring. Only one of this large family has flowers better than its leaves, the handsome tall species *A. lactiflora*. The rest are invaluable foliage plants. Some such as southernwood (*A. abrotanum*) grow up to four feet.

Somerset', a clear heliotrope pink, is extra smelly. So is the elegant 'Madame Calot' with pale pink and creamy white flowers. Scent is perhaps more pronounced amongst the doubles than the singles. If you look hard enough, you will find peonies that give you good autumn colour as well as June scent. 'Magic Orb' is a free-flowering double, heavily scented, with vivid rose outer petals guarding a jostle of cream and rose petals inside. The leaves colour orange and russet as the plant dies back in autumn. It is rather tall however and may not be the one to use with the rose in this particular scheme. Try and find a corner for it somewhere else.

The rose 'Blanche Double de Coubert' under which the peony is to be planted has chalk-white blooms, so the peony itself should probably not be white. Leave room around the base of the rose to pile on plenty of bulky mulch during winter or spring. The peony and the rose are such stars that you need only fill in round them with plants that will provide contrasts in foliage, and perhaps a flash of blue with a campanula such as *C. latiloba* 'Percy Piper' or the elegant *C. x burghaltii*. *C. lactiflora* 'Prichard's Variety' is less showy, but useful, if you are looking for something to fill in at the side of the rose. In spirit, campanulas are very close to peonies and roses, all of them denizens of cottage gardens and all cheerful, unfussy survivors. *C. latiloba* is more robust and coarse than the wiry-stemmed *C. persicifolia*. It makes a stronger splash of colour as all its flowers come out in June, whereas the other wobbles on in an indeterminate way, pushing out a few flowers here and there throughout the summer. *C. latiloba* holds its flowers tight against its stem. They open into wide bells, blue or white depending on the variety. The lance-shaped leaves make rosettes flat on the ground and last through the winter, unlike most others of the tribe. 'Percy Piper' has the habit of throwing outside stems when the main one has finished flowering. If you cut this out, the subsidiary growths extend the flowering period usefully. It grows about 3ft/90cm high and would be good alongside the peony. It runs a little, but not too aggressively. By nature, most campanulas are migrants, moving on to new pastures when they have exhausted the possibilities of their present site. *C. latifolia* is taller and less well groomed for the flower border, but it is strong and self-supporting. 'Brantwood' is one of the best forms, a deeper blue than the ordinary type. For a froth of ground cover round the front of this group, or between rose and campanula, use one of the neater kinds of artemisia, which with its grey foliage will tie together the other plants in this small June group, without distracting attention from them. The ancient cottage favourite, southernwood or lad's love, is too tall for this job. Something built on the lines of *A. schmidtiana* will be more suitable. This is a prostrate perennial with foliage finely cut into silver threads. It looks mothy in winter.

Many of the artemisias have dreary flowers, often muddy yellow which is not usually what you want in schemes with pink and magenta. There is only one answer : to cut them off as they appear. In *A. schmidtiana*'s case, this will not be until September, when they will avoid bumping noses with the peonies.

Plants for summer shade

The final scheme for June, in white, apricot and blue, is one for shade. Shade is usually cast as the delinquent of the garden scene ; difficult, gloomy and slow to respond to treatment. Town gardeners in particular moan about lack of sun in dank plots, but in gardening terms there is nothing wrong with shade. There are as many plants that like it as that don't. There is a luxuriance and mysteriousness about plants growing in shade which you never get in full sun. Reaction to it in the end depends on temperament. Shade is an introvert and favours white and blue. The flowers that most need the sun are extrovert reds and yellows : poppies, zinnias, sunflowers, red hot pokers. Of course, some shade is better than others and it changes according to the time of year. In the winter, one's whole garden may be cast into Stygian gloom. In the important growing season between April and August, however, the sun is much higher in the sky and light starts to filter through over roofs and between buildings in a most surprising way. Because of the angle at which light comes into the garden, a plant close to the ground may be in full shade, while a shrub 5ft/1.5m high may have its head in the sun. Shade caused by overhanging trees is less dense than the blocks of shadow thrown by tall buildings. Where there is tree shade, however, there are also tree roots guzzling away at the food and drink you might prefer your plants to have. The answer is to provide more than usual of both. Use lashings of long-lasting bonemeal in spring. Place rich collars of dung, leaf-mould, compost or whatever bulky material you can get hold of round your shrubs. Sprinkle a top dressing of fine mushroom compost or concentrated Cowpact or 6X manure round everything else. Many sun plants perform better when they are half starved. Shade plants do not. This scheme is made for a place that is shady, but not starved or dry.

The centrepiece is one of the wedding-cake viburnums, either *V. plicatum* 'Rowal-lane' or the shorter 'Mariesii'. Both grow in the same distinctive way, with wide-spreading branches in horizontal tiers. The flowers are white, like a lacecap hydrangea, and the leaves, though not outstanding, are handsome in an understated way. This is a shrub that needs plenty of space around it, so that its fine form is not muddled by other plants lolling into it. Resist the urge to prune it. If you cut one branch, it begins to look

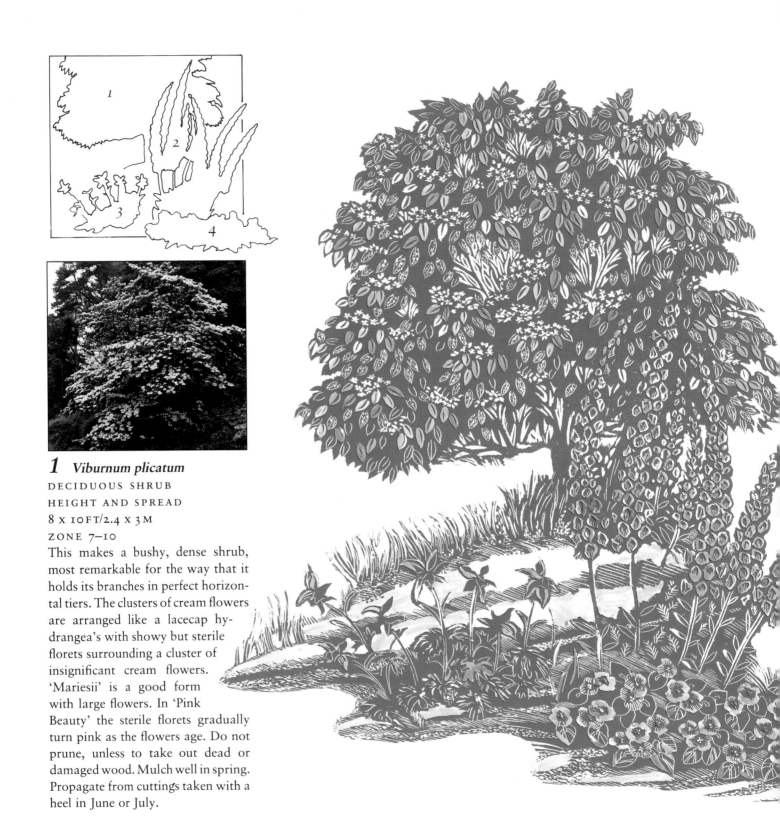

1 *Viburnum plicatum*

DECIDUOUS SHRUB
HEIGHT AND SPREAD
8 X 10FT/2.4 X 3M
ZONE 7–10

This makes a bushy, dense shrub, most remarkable for the way that it holds its branches in perfect horizontal tiers. The clusters of cream flowers are arranged like a lacecap hydrangea's with showy but sterile florets surrounding a cluster of insignificant cream flowers. 'Mariesii' is a good form with large flowers. In 'Pink Beauty' the sterile florets gradually turn pink as the flowers age. Do not prune, unless to take out dead or damaged wood. Mulch well in spring. Propagate from cuttings taken with a heel in June or July.

2 *Digitalis* 'Sutton's Apricot'
BIENNIAL
HEIGHT AND SPREAD
48 × 18IN/120 × 45CM
ZONE 5–9

Foxgloves have great elegance and charm and their strongly vertical outline lends substance to plantings of dumpier shrubs and perennials. Unfortunately the gorgeous variety 'Sutton's Apricot' is only biennial. The bells are lush and plentiful and fade to a paler colour at the edges. Sow seed as for aquilegias, between May and July, and thin out the plantlets if necessary. Move to permanent quarters in September and October, by which time the foxgloves should have made strong basal rosettes of leaves. They will shoot up to flower in summer of the following year. They thrive in semi-shade and moist, but not waterlogged, soil.

3 *Aquilegia* (Columbine, Granny's bonnet)
DECIDUOUS PERENNIAL
HEIGHT AND SPREAD
24 × 18IN/60 × 45CM
ZONE 3–9

A. alpina is one of the most desirable of this engaging family. It is smaller than the granny's bonnet (*A. vulgaris*) of cottage gardens and has elegant fern-like leaves topped by brilliant blue flowers, the petals pointed but without the long spurs that characterize many modern hybrids. *A. flabellata* is similar but

smaller in all its parts. All grow happily in semi-shade and are easily raised from seed. Take your cue from the plants, which are liberal self-seeders, and sow your seed between May and July, transferring plants to permanent quarters in September or October. They hybridize freely, so if you grow more than one type you may end up with a garden full of indeterminate, but always attractive progeny. Cut down stems after flowering if necessary.

4 *Viola*
EVERGREEN PERENNIAL
HEIGHT AND SPREAD
4 × 8IN/10 × 20CM
ZONE 5–9

This is a vast group, embracing the large monkey-faced pansies as well as tiny wildlings such as *V. odorata*. Some are more robust than others. The distinctive horn at the back of viola flowers is supposed to indicate how hardy they are. The longer the horn, the more optimistic you may be about its performance. 'Irish Molly' is supreme, a weird old gold/brown colour not found anywhere else among flowers: unfortunately it tends to flower itself to death. 'Baby Lucia' is a dwarf pansy with small deep blue flowers. They tolerate a wide range of soils. Cut back in autumn. Leggy plants can be cut back close to the ground and earthed up to encourage fresh shoots. Dead-head regularly to maintain the flow of flowers. Sow seed in mid- to late summer and transplant to permanent positions in autumn. Take cuttings from established plants in spring.

unbalanced. You cut another, like a bad barber, until it has scarcely any growth to call its own. Behind the viburnum at a suitable distance, use tall spires of foxgloves, preferably 'Sutton's Apricot', which you will almost certainly have to grow from seed. This will require forethought, but foxgloves are easy to raise and this particular one more than worth the trouble. Its name explains it. The bells are a most beautiful soft apricot. Like its wild relative, it is biennial, but unfortunately does not self-seed with the other's abandon. If you like the effect and want to perpetuate it, you must constantly raise new plants. If you have a wall or trellis behind the plot where you have put your viburnum centrepiece, trail a honeysuckle over it, which will pick up the warm pink-orange tones of the foxglove. The honeysuckle *L. x tellmanniana* is a gorgeous thing, yellow trumpets flushed with red. It is not as noticeably scented as other honeysuckles, although it puts on a decent attempt in the evenings, when the moths that pollinate it begin to fly. Any of the wilder types of honeysuckle would do instead, or perhaps *L. caprifolium*, a vigorous species with fragrant creamy flowers. In front of the viburnums, use clumps of something blue. Occasionally the brilliant blue flowers of the columbine *Aquilegia alpina* will hang on long enough to do the job, but in most seasons this species has packed its flowering bags by June. A blue-flowered strain of the ordinary granny's bonnet would be almost as good, but not quite so elegant. The effect of many of the blues is dissipated by their having white centres. The low-spreading *Omphalodes cappadocica* thrives in shade and has flowers of a most intense blue, but its foliage will not make such a contrast with the viburnum and foxglove as the aquilegia. To fill in along the front, use violas, either the neat, summer sky-coloured 'Boughton Blue' or rather more adventurously, the weird khaki 'Irish Molly', which will look ravishing with the viburnum and the foxgloves and which flowers happily in shade.

JULY

JULY IS THE SUPREME MONTH FOR P.G. WODEHOUSES 'FLARZE' THE lupins, delphiniums, campanulas, achilleas and monardas beloved of Blandings's ferocious gardener, Angus McAllister. It is the month of the herbaceous border and though few people have the great sheets of space that this style of gardening demands, it is still possible to get a suitably lush effect by putting together plants that have more than their flowers to contribute to the effect. In high summer it is easy to be dazzled by colour, but the most satisfying planting schemes will always have more than this to offer. Contrasts of form and foliage are of paramount importance. Many of the herbaceous plants that we use in the garden tend to have the same rounded, hummocky profile : cranesbills, astrantias, alchemilla, epimediums on the ground floor, phlox and its herbaceous border companions in the middle storey. Use the sword-like leaves of plants such as sisyrinchium and crocosmia to break up this potentially soporific outlook of low hills. Use an occasional monster such as onopordum or cardoon to change the proportions of your planting groups.

Leaf shape is almost as variable a characteristic as flower colour and you must learn to juggle with them both to get the best effects this month. Leaves have greater staying power. Romneya, for instance, flowers in July with large tissue-paper blooms of white with yellow eyes. It is a good flowerer and should go on producing until September. The leaves do even better, making a mound of deeply lobed, blue-grey foliage that is always pleasant to see and which will be with you for at least six months. Acanthus is also as valuable for its foliage as it is for its flowers. If you look in a plant dictionary, you find a bewildering number of names to describe leaf shapes, but all you need to hold in your mind is a series of rough groupings. Many hostas and the ground-covering bergenias have roughly the same rounded, fat, smooth leaves. Fennel has thread-like leaves, similar in style though not in colour to some of the filigree-leaved artemisias. Rodgersias have distinctive hand-shaped leaves. Use forms that contrast with one another, or use a leaf of good shape and substance to disguise the shortcomings of plants such as asters and most of the daisy family that have foliage that is at best undistinguished. A good foliage plant such as the smoke bush, cotinus, will also strengthen a planting of smaller, sparser flowering plants, providing the necessary bulk to flesh out their often puny frames.

Texture is another aspect of the leaf game that needs some thought. Shrubs such as choisya, camellia, aucuba, fatsia, holly and *Magnolia grandiflora* are useful in planting schemes because they are evergreen. They are also all glossy and the surface of their leaves reflects the light. This makes them appear more lively than the leaves of *Hydrangea aspera villosa* or the low-growing *Geranium renardii* which are both matt-textured. This is not to say that one is intrinsically better than the other. You need both. A garden composed entirely of glittering evergreens would be lacking in texture. A satin shirt does not look its most smooth and slippery against a satin jacket, but against dull grosgrain or fluffy wool. Some thickly textured leaf, such as the woolly willow, *Salix lanata*, will be enhanced by a neighbour such as choisya. The choisya will benefit too.

Leaf form and texture are not such immediately arresting characteristics as leaf colour and it is easy to get carried away by gold and silver, purple and variegated leaves in mixed plantings. Boldly coloured foliage needs to be used with care. A garden with too much is like a letter full of exclamation marks. Your eye is never allowed to travel far without being abruptly brought up short. This is tiring. Purple is, in many ways, the most difficult foliage colour to place. In summer, it becomes heavy, somehow depressing. Dust shows up reproachfully on the leaves of the purple-leaved nut. It is easier to use the colour in small touches : a pool of the glossy-leaved bugle lapping at the edge of alchemilla or hosta, a few clumps of the pretty purple-leaved violet, *Viola labradorica purpurea* or some of the floppy sedum 'Vera Jameson' with succulent bronze-purple stems and heads of grey-pink flowers.

Silver is one of the easiest colours to work unobtrusively into schemes. Of course, it is equally easy to overdo it, although it might seem the easiest way not to get things wrong. All grey gardens, or 'white' gardens as their defenders call them, are difficult to do well. There is a general consensus that greys indicate a gardener of taste but more greys do not necessarily equal more style. Lumped thoughtlessly together, they can have all the allure of last week's laundry. Many of them have the same matt, sometimes hairy texture, developed as a defence against sun in their Mediterranean homelands. You can, by using big-leaved verbascums and cabbagy *Salvia argentea*, introduce some variety of form, but many of the herbaceous greys – artemisias, achilleas, santolinas – have leaves similar in their fussiness. Leave the idea of the all-white/grey garden where it started, with Vita Sackville-West at Sissinghurst, and experiment instead with ways of using grey foliage in mixed plantings for July. Steely eryngiums will be useful allies.

Variegated plants are perhaps the most difficult to resist collecting. The patterns are as various as fingerprints : swirled, edged, blotched, spotted. Some plants, such as the leafy pulmonaria, streaked in silver, or the ground-covering lamiums, are very gently, recessively variegated. They do not draw too much attention to themselves. Others are brassily extrovert, like elaeagnus and the golden forms of *Euonymus fortunei*. Common sense dictates that you will be able to have more of the quiet than the noisy. If you choose a variegated plant for the ground level of your planting scheme, it would be as well to partner it with some rather plain plants above. If there is another extremely eye-catching plant at middle level, your gaze will be zooming up and down from one to the other, faster than an Otis elevator.

Deep purple

Plants with good foliage are used in this July planting scheme of yellow and blue, backed and drawn together by a purple cotinus, one of the best of all dark-leaved shrubs. In an island bed, the cotinus can be used as a central anchor, with clumps of the biennial evening primrose and baptisia, lilies and eryngium around it. If you are short of space, the same cotinus can be used as a background for the Japanese anemones, aster and sedum of September's planting scheme. Or you could enliven its bare outlines in March with generous plantings of crocus and scillas. If you are planting in a border against a wall, do not put the cotinus too close to the boundary. Left to its own devices, it is a pleasing, well-balanced shrub and it is a pity to cramp its style. If the border seems too narrow to accommodate the cotinus with all its July outriders, abandon it and cover that section of the boundary with a purple-leaved vine instead. If you want to be fanciful, it can be trained over a wide semi-circular arch rising above the boundary.

If you feel that you cannot live with purple leaves or think that they may be too dominant in a small garden, use the ordinary green-leaved *Cotinus coggygria* or its American cousin, *C. obovatus*, instead. Both have a haze of pale pink smoke around them all summer and both turn a vivid orange in the autumn, given suitable weather. The heaviness of the purple-leaved forms such as 'Notcutt's Variety' and 'Royal Purple' is transformed if the bush is planted so that you see it against the light. Viewed in this way, the foliage becomes translucent, like watered-down wine. Purple-leaved varieties need full sun if they are to develop decent colour. Others are quite happy growing in half shade.

Some purple-leaved varieties flower less well than others. 'Royal Purple' is less

1 *Cotinus coggygria*
(**Smoke tree**)
DECIDUOUS SHRUB
HEIGHT AND SPREAD
10 X 10FT/3 X 3M
ZONE 5–9

Distinctive rounded leaves are this shrub's hallmark, either bronze-green or rich purple. All types have brilliant autumn colour. Panicles of flowers, individually microscopic, are borne in July and their hazy appearance gives the shrub its common name. The best foliage comes from hard pruning in spring, but this will

be at the expense of the flowers. Cut out a few of the oldest growths each March. Propagate by layering shoots in April or take cuttings in May.

2 *Clematis*
(**Summer flowering**)
DECIDUOUS CLIMBER
HEIGHT AND SPREAD
VARIES WIDELY
ZONE 5–9

The three different ways of pruning roughly match up with the three periods of flowering. In July, you can stick to those kinds that need cutting back hard in February and early March. This includes all the Viticella varieties such as 'Abundance' and many others such as pale blue 'Ascotiensis' or 'Prins Hendrik'. Mulch liberally to keep the roots cool, well-fed and moist. Feed sandy soils with muck.

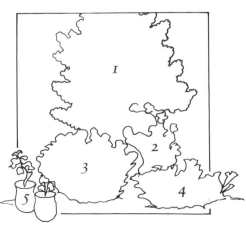

3 *Oenothera biennis* (Evening primrose)
BIENNIAL
HEIGHT AND SPREAD
3 X 1 FT/90 X 30 CM
ZONE 5–9

Philip Miller, curator of the Chelsea Physic Garden in the eighteenth century, dismissed this as 'a troublesome weed', but it is an attractive one, with tall stems carrying pale yellow scented flowers. It is a prolific self-seeder. In the first year, rosettes of leaves hug the ground. In the summer of its second year, the plant flowers. It thrives anywhere and is not fussy about soil. Plants can be raised from seed sown in a nursery row in June and planted out where they are to flower in September.

4 *Eryngium* (Sea holly)
DECIDUOUS OR EVERGREEN
BIENNIALS AND PERENNIALS
HEIGHT AND SPREAD
2 X 2 FT/60 X 60 CM or more
ZONE 6–10

The stiff, spiky outlines of all this family enhance any planting scheme, provided they have enough space round them to stand freely silhouetted. *E. alpinum* has the best flowers, a blue, thistly dome surrounded by a lacy ruff of gorgeous metallic blue. Most, except *E. giganteum*, flower from July to August. They like sun and well-drained soil. Cut flowered stems down to ground level in autumn. Propagate by dividing

clumps in August or by sowing seed in late March or April. It is tricky to get it to germinate. Mix seed with damp vermiculite in a polythene bag and keep it in a warm airing cupboard during January and February. Put the bag in the refrigerator during March and then sow on top of moist compost in a cool greenhouse or on a windowsill.

5 *Lilium* (Lily)
BULB
HEIGHT AND SPREAD
Varies widely
ZONE 6–9

In the wild, the martagon lily is one of the family's most successful colonizers, found in a great sweep of country from Portugal to Mongolia. It is also one of the most persistent of lilies. Bulbs, once settled, will last for decades. A deep, pinky mauve is the standard flower colour, but they can be dark purple or white, all quite small and swept back into Turks' caps. The fresh green leaves are held in whorls round the stem. Lilies hate to be disturbed, so it is worth spending time getting their home right. Adequate humus and good drainage will make them happy. *L. regale* with white trumpet flowers is one of the easiest and therefore best known of lilies. When growing well, it can get up to 6ft/1.8m. Plant in autumn or spring and mulch annually in spring with well-rotted compost. Protect against underground slugs with regular doses of molluscicide.

good in this respect than 'Foliis Purpureis', though it has excellent foliage, deep purplish-red. Hard pruning each spring results in extra-good foliage produced on new growth, but you sacrifice the smoke, which is only produced on wood that is three or four years old. You can balance the two effects by judiciously thinning out some of the old wood, perhaps up to a third, each spring to stimulate new growth. The remaining two-thirds can then grow on and flower in the normal way.

If space is short and you are trying to cram as many plants as possible into this July scheme, try running a pale blue clematis through the cotinus. 'Perle d'Azur' would do well, or the vigorous 'Mrs Cholmondeley' which gives a stunning performance in July and then continues to produce odd flowers on new growth for the rest of the summer. These will not suit tidy-minded gardeners, who perhaps should choose their clematis from the group that can be cut down hard every February. The large-flowered 'Ascotiensis', bright lavender blue with greenish stamens, might do, or the equally lovely 'Huldine' with white, mauve-backed petals. When you are planting clematis to grow through a shrub, do not jam it up against the main stem of the host, where they will have to fight each other for food and water. Set the clematis at least 18in/45cm away from the trunk of its companion and train the first growths in on a slanting bamboo cane. Once it has made contact with its host, it will hang on single-mindedly, curling its leaf stalks round any protuberance it can find. Clematis are at their best growing through other plants. They are not, in themselves, plants of grace or stature. When grown in isolation, splayed against trellis, you are very conscious of their top-heaviness, a bundle of leaves and flowers up above the first-floor windows and a dry-looking set of bare spindly stems from ground- to eye-level. Flowers are the clematis's only asset ; much better to let it borrow substance and support from another shrub and disguise its own shortcomings. The flowers will always float to the surface, so you need not worry that they will be buried by a jealous host-shrub.

Aspect is less important than fodder. Clematis look as ethereal as ballet dancers, but have appetites like prize fighters. Constant mulching with well-rotted muck will not only feed, but also keep the underlying soil cool and damp. Thin, sandy soils will need some bulking up if clematis are to grow well. Mulching will also dissuade you from scrabbling around or weeding too close to the clematis's brittle stems. Dogs and children will already be queuing up to snap the stems for you. It seems a pity to do it yourself.

Beside the cotinus, set plants of the evening primrose, *Oenothera biennis*. If fresh plants are put in for the first two years, there will for ever after be a permanent supply. They are eager self-seeders, but not too greedy of space during the first year when, like actors, they rest, working up to the great performance. Some gardeners dismiss the plant as unrefined, but it is a hearty doer, prolific with its soft yellow saucer flowers and wonderfully scented in the evening. Each flower opens from a pointed, slightly red-tinged bud and the process is riveting, like a speeded-up film. Silently, but rather jerkily, the petals unfurl, shedding the tight green bud wrapping, and arrange themselves in an orderly circle, each of the four, 1in/2.5cm-long petals overlapping the next. The flowers open in succession from the bottom to the top of a tall spike. They do not last long, but because there are so many of them, this does not matter. If you turn up your nose at something so common, try *Oenothera tetragona* instead. This is perennial, but does not grow to such a splendid branching size as the biennial version. It stops at about 2ft/ 60cm and has denser spikes of flowers, a brighter, more buttery yellow than *O. biennis*, whose tissue-paper flowers are a soft, milky yellow.

Close to these, grow clumps of the handsome but unusual perennial *Baptisia australis*. This is a great plant : glaucous, pea-like foliage on sturdy stems up to 3ft/ 90cm tall, topped with spikes of rich indigo-blue pea flowers. For safety's sake it should have a corset of pea-sticks to keep it in shape. It is also a greedy plant. Give it lashings of mulch each autumn and a handful of something explosively nitrogenous each spring. Its name comes from the Greek word meaning to dye. Where true indigo was hard to come by, this North American substitute was used instead. In the wild it is found on neutral or fairly acid soil, but will thrive in gardens in a wide variety of soils, provided they are well drained and the plant is in full sun. It hates to be disturbed. Like the vetch and other members of the pea family, it sets seeds in scimitar-shaped seed-pods, in this case, dark grey. They can be dried on the stem and used in winter arrangements.

For a marbled sheet of foliage to tuck around the feet of the baptisia and evening primrose, choose *Eryngium variifolium*, a reasonably hardy evergreen variety with tough, curled dark green leaves, boldly veined in white. The flowers, thistle-shaped, each surrounded by six stiff bracts, are not as showy as other eryngiums, but provide a useful grey-blue effect from midsummer to early autumn. When the flower head has finished its act, new leaves start sprouting from the base and lie very flatly against the ground. *E. amethystinum* is not variegated but has more thickly branching stems and bluer flowers, backed by dark blue bracts, showier than *E. variifolium*, though the leaves are not so good. *E. alpinum* has the biggest flower heads, cone-shaped and surrounded by a complicated ruff of blue bracts and spines. All these are perennials, but the popular Miss Willmott's ghost, *E. giganteum*, is biennial, producing flat green rosettes of leaves one year and widely branched heads of metallic silvery flowers the next. It seeds itself about freely. As their common name, sea holly, suggests, they are natives of dunes and shingle beaches and demand good drainage.

When you can afford it, plant clumps of lilies amongst the other plants. It is scarcely worth buying one lily bulb on its own. Five are good, ten more than twice as good. Even ten will not cost more than a couple of bottles of wine and the intoxication will last much longer. Getting a lily to flower in its first year is no problem. When you have brought it successfully through its second year, you can award yourself a merit star. When you buy a lily (with all the usual caveats : from a reputable supplier, etc. etc.) its first season's flowers will already be formed in embryo and you will have to be determinedly crass to prevent that flower leaping out in summer. Drainage is probably the single most potent cause of failure in successive seasons. Lilies demand good drainage, but they also hate drying out. Heavy clay soils are the most difficult to convert to suitable des. res. We all tend to cheat on the boring work of excavating heavy land, but lilies will not forgive you for skimping. On heavy ground, you will need to incorporate bags and bags of leaf-mould, or peat mixed with bonemeal. Lay each lily bulb on a bed of sharp sand and sprinkle more sand into the mixture that you use to fill up the planting hole. Sharp sand is the term for a particularly rough, gritty sand : ordinary builder's stuff will not do. Most lilies prefer a soil that is just the acid side of neutral. *Lilium auratum*, *L. pardalinum*, and *L. speciosum* and its cultivars are the fussiest. The martagon lilies are perfectly happy on limy soils and the subdued purple martagon would be a good choice for this July scheme. The flowers are quite small, but there are a lot of them, with petals swept back into Turk's caps, borne in spikes about 4ft/120cm tall. The most common form is a strange brownish-purple with bright ginger stamens, but there is an elegant pure white form too. The narrow leaves grow in whorls up the stems.

The well-known regale lily would fit well into the planting scheme, too. It is a relatively undemanding flower, anxious to do its best. It has white, funnel-shaped blooms with yellow throats, the petals washed on the outside with pinkish-purple. It has a powerful sweet scent – better than that of the martagon, which smells worse than a badger's sett. It also has the advantage of being among the cheapest of lily bulbs. If it does disappear suddenly from your planting scheme, it will not be quite so painful as losing a bulb of *L. auratum platiphyllum*, six times the price. *L. regale album* is as reliable as its parent and has the same long trumpet-shaped flowers, but they are pure white inside and out. 'Snowstar' is about the same height with wide, upward-facing flowers. They splay open from long, upright buds. The stamens, with their wobbling loads of pollen protrude showily above the petals.

As to position, lilies like the clematis formula : feet in shade, head in sun. They are ideal for growing through the low branches of shrubs that can provide a parasol of leaves to keep the sun off their roots. Low shrubby growth will also help to anchor lilies safely, though they should never be planted where they will catch the worst of the prevailing wind. Some, such as the easy-going martagons, thrive in the light dappled shade cast by taller shrubs. Deep shade suits none of them.

Plant sculpture

July is often the hottest month of the year, when the garden is likely to be lived in as much as the house. Particularly spectacular schemes are called for to be admired from deckchair, hammock and terrace. The pieces of garden that you can see most easily from kitchen or sitting room should perhaps be saved for spring and autumn planting schemes, when you will not so easily be tempted out of doors. Summer schemes can rampage farther from the house, with tubs and pots spilling with annuals or more lilies on paving next to the house. Exotic plants such as phormiums, cordylines, astelia and aeoniums are also excellent in tubs and pots and bring an air of the Mediterranean and faraway New Zealand to a domestic patch. None of them are fully hardy, but if you have some protected place – a lean-to greenhouse, porch or conservatory – where they can overwinter, this need not be a problem. They are good in town gardens, or where there is a lot of paving. There, their outlandish, distinctly un-British personalities can dominate the stage. The phormiums have leathery, sword-like leaves and long branched panicles of flowers that last from July to September. The variety *P. tenax purpureum* has dark bronze foliage and flowers of an orangey-bronze. It looks excellent with the curry plant, *Helichrysum angustifolium*, which has silver-grey needles of leaves and smells hotter than a vindaloo, or with the broad-leaved *Helichrysum petiolare* 'Limelight'. All the helichrysums look good with phormiums. Both plants are equally foreign-looking and both adapt happily to pot life. Although the species *Phormium tenax* grows naturally up to an overpowering 10ft/3m, the hybrids are easier to manage. 'Bronze Baby' is only 2ft/60cm high, with bold wine-red foliage standing in stiff swords. 'Dazzler' is bigger and more complicated. The leaves are striped along their length with yellow, salmon-pink, orange and bronze, but you cannot exactly tell when one colour has merged into the next. The general impression is of pink-bronze, quite unlike any leaf produced by English plants. Cordyline, like phormium, is a New Zealander, with a similar spiky silhouette. Whereas phormiums are strongly vertical, the lower leaves of cordylines splay out to make a perfect half-sphere of foliage. Left to itself in warm climates, it will make

1 *Acanthus* (Bear's breeches)

DECIDUOUS PERENNIAL
HEIGHT AND SPREAD
4 X 4 FT/120 X 120 CM
ZONE 6–9

In a mild winter, acanthus does not die back completely, but keeps a skeleton supply of leaves going to remind you of its splendour in high summer. *A. spinosus* has deeply cut leaves up to 2ft/60cm long, in glossy dark green. *A. mollis* has cabbagy leaves, equally glossy, but giving more bulk. It rarely flowers as freely as *A. spinosus*. It prefers full sun and needs regular mulching with some heavily nitrogenous muck to stimulate a good supply of leaves. In a drought summer, it may suffer from mildew.

2 *Romneya coulteri* (Tree poppy)

DECIDUOUS SUB-SHRUB
HEIGHT AND SPREAD
4 X 4 FT/90 X 90 CM
ZONE 8–10

Although difficult to establish, the Californian poppy is a romper, if it gets over its initial shyness. Both foliage and flowers are handsome, the former glaucous grey, deeply lobed and cut, the latter papery-white up to 5in/12cm across, each with a brilliant central boss of gold stamens. Reasonably hardy, once established, but will need winter protection in the north. Plant in April and May in a light, well-drained soil in a sheltered spot. Cut down stems to a few inches above ground level in October. In the north, cover the base of the plant with bracken or fern fronds, weathered ashes or peat. Propagate by digging up suckers, which may bob up some distance from the parent plant. 'White Cloud' is a hybrid with larger flowers and is the best garden variety. It is a hybrid of two species, *R. coulteri* and *R. tricocalyx*.

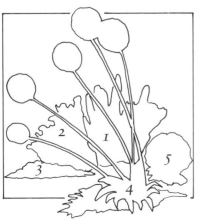

3 *Phalaris arundinacea* 'Picta' (Gardeners' garters)

DECIDUOUS PERENNIAL

HEIGHT AND SPREAD

3FT/90CM X INDEFINITE

ZONE 6–9

This grass has a desperate desire to overrun its neighbours and needs dealing with regularly and strictly. It has long ribbon leaves, striped longitudinally in cream and pale green. Insignificant feathery heads of creamy-green flowers are borne in June and July. It will grow in any soil in sun or shade and needs no special feeding. The easiest way to keep it within bounds is to trench round it in early autumn and dig up any growths that come outside this cordon sanitaire. If you cut it down at the end of July, new growth will appear, looking rather fresher than the old. Increase by division (if you dare) in autumn or spring.

4 *Allium*

DECIDUOUS BULB

HEIGHT AND SPREAD

Varies with species

ZONE 6–8

The typically spherical heads of the summer-flowering onions are made up of masses of tiny star-shaped flowers, purple with a metallic sheen in *A. albopilosum*, which grows 12–15in/30–38cm high. This dries as it ages to a stiff skeleton lollipop, almost as effective in death as it was alive. *A. giganteum* is much taller and has more densely packed heads of purple flowers. The thin strappy leaves have a grey tinge and droop at the ends. They are susceptible to early spring frosts. Find a sheltered spot for it. They both like an open sunny

situation and well-drained soil. Heavy soil can be improved with coarse sand or grit, mixed in the planting hole. Increase by dividing clumps of bulbs in spring. Do not cut back the foliage, but allow it to die down naturally. It feeds goodness back into the bulbs for the next season.

5 *Nigella damascena* (Love-in-a-mist)

HARDY ANNUAL

HEIGHT AND SPREAD

24 X 8IN/60 X 20CM

ZONE 5–9

Introduced from Damascus more than four hundred years ago, this has remained a popular cottage-garden flower. It has light feathery foliage and flowers usually of blue, as in the excellent variety 'Miss Jekyll'. There is a low-growing variety 'Dwarf Moody Blue' only 6–8 in tall but it is not as elegant as the standard varieties. Nor are colour mixtures as effective as the plain blue. Swollen seed pods are a great feature at the end of the season and can be cut, dried and used in decorations inside. Seed can be sown where the plants are to flower. Prepare the seedbed carefully, breaking down lumps of soil, and sow the seed thinly at the beginning of April. Cover with a fine scattering of soil and protect with netting if necessary. Thin the seedlings as they emerge, if they are overcrowded to allow them to develop properly.

a small tree, each long upright stem finishing in a spiky topknot of foliage. There is no danger of this happening in the average British back yard. Try one of the bronze varieties such as *C. australis* 'Atropurpurea' in a pot with the metallic silver leaves of *Convolvulus cneorum* arranged around its feet.

Astelia is a New Zealander with thick, grass-like leaves and a liking for hot spots. It is a member of the lily family, but its garden value lies in its leaves rather than its flowers, which are small, rising in short spikes from the centre of the rosettes of leaves. The growth is open and arching, less spikily upright than the phormiums. The lustre on the leaves, like polished pewter, catches and reflects the light in a pleasing way. They grow best in full sun, or only slightly dappled shade, in any decent soil that is not too dry. They are evergreen, if given the chance, and will not overwinter without protection, but give a pleasantly outlandish touch to a July planting. The variety *A. nivicola* 'Red Gem' has lustrous red-green foliage overlaid with a silvery sheen. *A. chathamica* 'Silver Spear' has a silvered leaf, growing about 2ft/60cm long. Use them in tubs on their own, or with a foreground planting of osteospermums or purple aeoniums.

Acanthus is a superb foliage plant for July, provided you have room for it. It is rather a grand thing and will not take kindly to being emasculated by gardeners who suddenly get frightened by its bulk. *Acanthus spinosus* has the most interesting leaves, dark, glossy green, long, relatively narrow and so deeply cut that each leaf looks as if it is made up of a series of holly leaves arranged along the midribs. The leaves die back in autumn and are relatively late to emerge in spring. Tall spikes of hooded flowers, white and purplish blue are borne on thick stems in July and August. Although the colour fades from them gradually, they still make a fine sculptural show, standing well clear of the mound of leaves. The problem when using it in a mixed planting scheme is that you always plant its companions too close to it, forgetting what an enormous spread the leaves have when they are fully grown. Then the neighbours get squashed, for there is little in the herbaceous line that can stand up to an acanthus once the bit is between its teeth. It is slow to settle into new ground and, conversely, is almost impossible to get rid of, once it has got going. It has plump, fleshy, deep roots which inevitably snap when you are heaving a plant out of the ground. These pieces, effectively root cuttings, gaily sprout the next spring, and you have not one big acanthus plant, but five small ones. If the patch in which you are planning to put your acanthus is backed by a fence or a wall, cover it with the pineapple broom, *Cytisus battandieri*, named after Jules Battandier, a French botanist whose speciality was the plants of North Africa. This one is a Moroccan and is a most un-broom-like broom in flower and leaf. The leaves are made up of three spoon-shaped silvery leaflets and have the dull, lustrous texture of expensive satin. To the touch, they are equally cool and slippery and the colour is olive-silver, more silver than olive on the youngest leaves. When they catch the light, they shine as brightly as metal. They are as important a part of the shrub's appearance as the flowers, which is just as well, for in July the leaves are all you will have. The dense domes of bright yellow flowers, smelling exotically of pineapple, appear in May and June. This shrub is evergreen if allowed to be by winter weather, but the growth tends to be lanky, with the best foliage on the ends of the branches. It is not reliably hardy, as you would expect of a Moroccan, and may be a gamble in cold gardens. A wall gives extra protection and the lax growths are easy to train and tie in. Where it is happy, this broom will grow up to 15ft/4.5m and spread over another 12ft/3.6m.

If you are short of space, forget the acanthus and plant romneya instead. Where it is suited, it will run around faster than a speed-crazed mole, but it can be difficult to establish. Again, the leaves are a great asset, more glaucous, waxy, than the broom's, absorbing rather than reflecting the light, but a superb pale blue-green foil for the huge poppy flowers of crumpled white tissue paper that appear from July to September. The standard version, *R. coulteri*, is vigorous, once it has decided whether it will stay with you at all, and can spread to 6ft/1.8m in any direction. A new variety, 'White Cloud', is more compact with the same fine foliage.

Fill in with the stripy grass, *Phalaris arundinacea* 'Picta' (but only if you are prepared to lift and replant it each autumn to prevent it throttling the whole scheme) and groups of one of the large-flowered globular alliums, *A. albopilosum* or *A. giganteum*. These start flowering in June, but the heads remain spectacular throughout the summer, balanced improbably on tall straight stems. When the bulbs come up to flower, the foliage goes to pieces, so it is as well to plant them where the romneya's foliage can loll comfortably over the alliums' and cover its scrappiness. Bulbs are usually available in autumn and need to be planted as soon as you can get hold of them. They like good drainage, so if your soil is heavy and damp, mix some coarse, gritty sand into the planting holes. *A. giganteum* has slightly nesh foliage, susceptible to late spring frosts. If you know your garden is a frost pocket, go for *A. albopilosum* instead. This has metallic purple flower heads which dry as they age to stiff spiny balls, but, at 12in/30cm high, is nowhere near as tall as *A. giganteum*. The alliums all belong to the onion tribe and 'require a fat ground well digged and dunged' as Gerard said in his sixteenth century *Herball*, one of the earliest gardening books. He would never have seen *A. giganteum*, introduced from Central Asia towards the end of the nineteenth century, but the European species *A.*

sphaerocephalum would have been familiar. It is much less showy than *A. giganteum*, growing to about half the height with dense, spherical heads, deep purple. They are highly rated by bumble bees, who sway about on them like acrobats on teeter boards.

A foreground of the annual love-in-a-mist, *Nigella damascena* will provide a romantic sky-blue haze but you need a good patch of them to make any impression ; taken alone, they are exceedingly wispy with thread-like foliage and pale blue flowers. The seed-pods are the most positive thing about them. They swell up into extraordinary pale green bladders, which gradually fade to a cream-buff colour. The old variety 'Miss Jekyll' is still one of the best. Sow seed directly into the ground where you want the flowers, when the soil has warmed up in early April.

Foliage to the fore

The final scheme for July is in shades of white, lime green and yellow and with a little juggling of components can be adapted for sun or shade. There is no shortage of candidates for this high-summer scheme : white lychnis, phlox or Shasta daisies, and white violas or the ever-useful low ground cover *Epilobium glabellum* for the bottom storey, yellow day-lilies or achillea, golden rod, loosestrife and thalictrum, lime-coloured tobacco flowers and feathery plumes of alchemilla filling in lower down. Variegated privet can act as a fulcrum, with the elegant, aromatic ginger mint echoing its yellow and green foliage at a lower level. Bronze fennel or the bronze-leaved crocosmia 'Solfaterre' will fit easily into this palette of colours. The weird green-flowered plantain *Plantago major* 'Rosularis' can also find a place here, well to the fore where its light green rosette flowers have some chance of being noticed. Start first with a centrepiece, something leafy to give substance to what is essentially a herbaceous scheme. Privet has long been despised as suburban, but its variegated form, *Ligustrum ovalifolium* 'Aureum' is a vigorous evergreen shrub, with glossy mid-green leaves, broadly margined in yellow. It will look best in a scheme like this if it is loosely kept to a formal shape – a shape that goes up rather than out, if you want to have plenty of room for planting around it. If you aspire to something rather smarter than privet in your back garden, think about the golden-leaved hop, *Humulus lupulus* 'Aureus'. If there is not a wall or fence for it to scramble over, you will have to give it some support to climb on, perhaps a tall, narrow trellis pyramid to make a centrepiece for this planting. There are plenty of designers waiting to run you up such a thing. The only difficulty may be the bill. The hop is not evergreen like the privet, but it has fine vine-like leaves in a soft greenish-yellow. There are hanging clusters of dry, papery hops in early autumn if you are lucky.

White phlox will shine out with some intensity against this background and though they start in July, will continue in flower through to September. Think of them as greedy dowagers. They look elegant and aristocratic, but need a great deal of feeding on the quiet. Five flowering stems to a clump is about as much as you should allow if you want decent heads of bloom. With them, grow lime-green tobacco flowers, which you will have to raise each year from seed. You may be lucky in your trawl through the bedding plants at the garden centre in spring, but the plants usually offered are mixtures such as the dwarf 'Domino', mostly pinks and purples, which will not give the same effect at all. Look for *Nicotiana* 'Lime Green' or the more unusual species *N. langsdorfii* which has branching stems of small lime-coloured flowers. Height may dictate choice. *N. langsdorfii*, when well-grown, can zoom up to 5ft/1.5m. 'Lime Green' hovers around half that height, and has showier flowers. The most important point in this scheme is to keep a balance between the three colours. To this end, if you need another plant to furnish the middle ground, use something yellow, perhaps a day-lily such as *Hemerocallis citrina* which has lemon-yellow trumpet flowers during July and August.

The bottom storey should be filled with alchemilla, if you have not already used it in your planting scheme for June, and perhaps the variegated ginger mint, *Mentha x gentilis* 'Variegata' which forms a mat of oval green leaves brightly spotted and striped in yellow. The leaves are aromatic, like the cooking herb, and it will grow as happily in shade as sun. Unimportant whorls of mauve flowers appear in summer. Its underground runners can be invasive, but it is reasonably easy to pull up. Fill in with an unlikely member of the willow herb family, *Epilobium glabellum*, a semi-evergreen perennial that grows no more than 8in/20cm high. Clumps of oval mid-green leaves are topped by small cup-shaped white flowers which unobtrusively do their bit from June to September. Creamy violas ('Moonlight' or 'Little David') and the green plantain are desirable extras.

1 Ligustrum ovalifolium 'Aureum' (Golden privet)

EVERGREEN SHRUB
HEIGHT AND SPREAD
12 X 10FT/3.6 X 3M
ZONE 6–9

Leaves are oval, glossy, mid-green, heavily margined with yellow. Dense clusters of white flowers open in mid-summer, but are not a great asset. Gertrude Jekyll used this golden privet in her main flower border at Munstead Wood with rue, verbascum and white everlasting pea. There is a similar, even more handsome variegated privet, but more difficult to find, *L. lucidum* 'Excelsum Superbum.' The large leaves are margined and mottled with yellow and cream. It never gets as big as the commoner golden privet, and can easily be trained as a topiary pyramid. If you decide to train it, it will need clipping at least twice a year in May and September. The variegated tones will develop most effectively in full sun. It needs no special feeding. Propagate by hardwood cuttings, 12in/30-cm long sections of seasoned growth, taken in October. Plant out the rooted cuttings in a nursery bed during the following April or May. Set the plants out in October.

2 Phlox paniculata

DECIDUOUS PERENNIAL
HEIGHT AND SPREAD
4 X 2FT/120 X 60CM
ZONE 4–9

Good, moist soil, slightly on the heavy side, pleases border phloxes. All are fully hardy and bear dense heads of flowers in late summer from July to September. 'Fujiyama' is a distinctive variety with cylindrical heads of washing-powder white on sturdy stems. 'White Admiral' has shapely heads of equally pure white. Staking with pea-sticks may be necessary in exposed situations. Mulch with well-rotted manure or

compost each spring and cut flower stems down to the ground each autumn. They will need splitting and replanting every few years. Do this in October or March. Get rid of all the woody growth and replant only the rigorous new pieces growing round the sides of the clump. You can also grow from seeds sown in March or April. Eelworm is a menace. If it strikes, burn diseased stock after propagating it from root cuttings taken in February or March.

3 *Nicotiana alata* (Tobacco plant)

PERENNIAL TREATED AS
HALF-HARDY ANNUAL
HEIGHT AND SPREAD
2 X 1 FT/60 X 30CM
ZONE 6–10

In rich well-drained soil, these are easy plants, wonderfully scented, particularly in the evening. 'Lime Green' is very prolific with its oddly coloured flowers and is easy to raise from seed. Sow in late March or early April, leaving the seeds uncovered on top of the compost. Maintain a temperature of 65–70°F/18–20°C during germination, which usually takes between two and three weeks. Prick off the seedlings and harden off before planting out in May.

4 *Alchemilla mollis* (Lady's mantle)

DECIDUOUS PERENNIAL
HEIGHT AND SPREAD
20 X 20IN/50 X 50CM
ZONE 4–9

Useful (though that is often a damning word in the plant world), clump-forming ground-cover plant with rounded, scalloped leaves of a downy texture. They hold raindrops in a most endearing way, each drop rounded like a bead of mercury. Sprays of tiny greenish-yellow flowers are carried through the summer, more froth than substance. Sometimes a late cold spell burns the edges of the leaves and stops them

opening fully; cut these off. They look painful and removing them will encourage fresh ones to grow. It is fully hardy and grows in any soil, in sun or shade. Cut back to the ground in autumn. Propagating will take care of itself, as alchemillas are prolific self-seeders. Seedlings are remarkably tenacious when anchoring themselves to the ground.

5 *Mentha x gentilis* 'Variegata' (Ginger mint)

DECIDUOUS PERENNIAL
HEIGHT AND SPREAD
18 X 24IN/45 X 60CM
ZONE 6–9

Charming, though slightly invasive ground cover, spreading, like ordinary mint, by stout underground runners. It has bright, fresh variegated foliage. It is unfussy about soil and will grow in sun or semi-shade, though its colour will be brighter in sun. It is happier in a damp soil. Plant at any time and propagate by digging up some of the outlying roots.

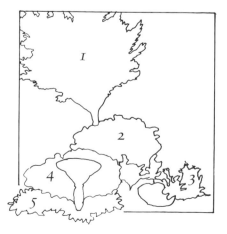

AUGUST

Nothing too arduous should be expected from the gardener in August: a little dead-heading perhaps, a little work with the water sprinkler and a great deal of contemplation from deckchair or hammock. August planting schemes should be planned for places where they can easily be admired from a prone position. Although August weather is all too often wet and overcast, we persist in thinking of it as an archetypal summer month. Certainly, if you have children at school, this will be the month when you are most likely to take a summer break. If this is a long one, then you may feel you can leave August out of your planting calendar altogether. If it is not, you would be wise to choose plants for this month that can be relied on to behave themselves in your absence. History does not relate whether Mikhail Bakunin, the Russian revolutionary, was also a gardener, but if he was not he should have been, for plants could teach him a thing or two about anarchy. You expect the grass to look awful on your return from a holiday. It always does, unless you have stored up a great string of favours done to friends and relatives and can persuade one of them to mow in your absence. You even expect some insurrection in the vegetable plot, with runner beans creeping off their poles to stifle the artichokes and courgettes, responding to some deeply atavistic call to arms, sweeping off the course you had so carefully planned for them and plunging into the lettuce bed instead.

What you do not expect, while you are lying supine far from home, is that the flower garden will rise up and have its own wild holiday, free from bondage and free from the hoe. Verbascums, which you may have left looking as stately and upright as any grand duke, will inevitably have snapped their stakes (if they ever were staked) and will be lolling drunkenly in all directions, crushing many small hopeful ground coverers, pansies, pinks and the like in the process. Roses, which before your departure looked as pretty as a Helen Allingham picture, have now developed long, whippy growths that with every lash seem to shriek 'Yah ! Booh ! Sucks !' as they demonstrate what a temporary illusion the order of the garden is. You do not willingly want to add to the insurgents' army with your August plantings. Grasses, still vastly underrated as components in mixed planting schemes, will be staunch allies in your battle for supremacy.

It is unfortunate that our early conditioning with hoes and lawn mowers should lead us to think of grass as an enemy. There are at least nine thousand different species in the world – not all of them bad. Stipa, miscanthus, glyceria, the blue lyme grass (elymus), helictotrichon are all suitable for the August garden. By nature, grasses have a graceful way of growing, even before any seed-heads appear. The leaves of some of the large varieties arch outwards like fountains. The dry rustling sound that they make in the slightest breeze is as calming and cooling as the sound of water dropping into a pool and a great deal cheaper to arrange. The chief difficulty you are likely to experience with grasses lies not in growing them, but in getting your mouth round some of the names. Hakonechloa and arrhenatherum sound as though they have been spat from a half-chewed dictionary and many of the plants in this large and diverse family have not been around long enough in gardens to acquire common names that we can use instead. Certainly, many are more difficult to pronounce than grow. They are not a fussy race, which is why, in evolutionary terms, they have been so successful. In size they vary enormously. The vast plumes of pampas grow 12ft/3.6m high and this is not a grass that can easily be used in mixed plantings. At the other end of the scale are the neat fescues, growing like clumps of blue-grey thrift, rarely more than 12in/30cm tall. When you use grasses such as the tall curving miscanthus in mixed plantings, take care that other plants are not packed too close to them. For these bigger grasses to show off their form they need space around them.

Bowles's golden grass, *Carex elata* 'Aurea', is strictly not a grass at all, but a sedge. As far as the gardener is concerned, the differences are minimal. The useful thing about the carex family is that they like damp, even wet soil, where many grasses would rot. Bowles's sedge has leaves of very rich golden yellow, each with a thin green margin. It is dramatic and tidy, a rather rare combination. It clumps up slowly and though the narrow leaves may be more than 1ft/30cm long, they arch gently outwards so that the general impression is of a lower plant, certainly one for foreground planting. Blackish-brown flower spikes appear in summer on triangular-shaped stems, the sedges' chief distinguishing characteristic. Useful ground cover, but vivid, so that its companions need to be chosen with care. It is fully hardy but must have moist soil. In deep shade, the colour may fade to yellowish-green. Increase by dividing clumps in spring.

Blue lyme grass, *Elymus arenarius*, is not so well-behaved. It is related to couch, public enemy number one in most gardens, and has similar aggressive tendencies. It is far more handsome, though, steely-blue with broader blades than couch and stiff, compact flower heads produced between June and August. It is used in conservation work to stabilize sand dunes, which it does with a fast-growing network of underground stolons. These are what you need to curb at regular intervals. This grass was a particular favourite of Gertrude Jekyll's. She used it with seakale in her grand mixed borders at Munstead Wood. Her method was to cut it down to ground level as it began to flower. She was happy to sacrifice the flower heads for the sake of a fresh crop of foliage in midsummer.

Large-leaved plants such as hostas and ligularias make excellent foliage contrasts with grasses. Plain green hostas would be a restful choice, perhaps the glossy pale green *H. plantaginea* that has spires of scented white flowers during August and September. *H. ventricosa* flowers earlier with spikes of mauve, but has equally good leaves, broadly ovate with a glaucous finish. As they are now container-grown, it is an easy matter to choose between varieties. Unfortunately, slugs dote on them. Be prepared to defend your plants as they emerge from the ground in late spring. If you use a variegated hosta with your grasses, remember that they keep their colour better in shade than sun.

The ligularias, like the carex, prefer damp soil, and all flower between July and August. Some have tall spires of small yellow flowers as in *L. przewalskii*, others much harsher, larger daisy flowers of vivid orange, as in the better known 'Desdemona'. *L. przewalskii* (you must pray you are never called upon to say the name out loud) has superb foliage, deeply cut and such a dark green that in some lights it appears purple. 'Desdemona' also has dark leaves but they are heart-shaped. They are dramatic plants, happy in sun or half shade, but they will not thrive in dry, sandy soils. Mulch them well each spring.

Colour should also be paramount in August. There is colour in grasses, as with *Milium effusum aureum*, which glows out of a semi-shaded corner. There are some good tawny coppers, too, among the sedges, such as *Carex buchananii*. Grass colours, however, are on the downbeat side of the palette. There should be plenty of the other sort of colour too : rich orange of marigolds and lilies, blue of agapanthus and delphinium, red of penstemon and *Lychnis chalcedonica*. If the colours clash, make sure they clash well, extrovertly, with panache. Of course it is safer to dabble in greys and whites and pinks. You cannot go wrong there, in the same way that you are told you cannot go wrong if you always wear beige. How sad, though, to go from cradle to grave, safely wrapped in beige. Better to experiment, even if the results are unexpected.

Several of the plants that have become popular in summer gardens – diascias, penstemons, felicias, osteospermums, argyranthemums, salvias – are not reliably hardy. This should not deter any but the most faint-hearted. If you have a cold frame or greenhouse, plants can be lifted and stored for the winter under cover. If space is limited, take cuttings from the parent plants and overwinter them inside. A windowsill will be enough. The full-grown plants can then be left to take their chance outside. Much will depend on where they are growing. Many town gardens are warmer than country ones. It must be the effect of all the central heating. In such sheltered microclimates, even tender felicias will come through a winter unscathed. These slightly tender perennials are far too good to abandon entirely. If cuttings and cold frames seem too much fuss, then think of this group as annuals and replace them each year in early June.

Gambling with exotics

Both penstemon and salvia are used in this first planting scheme for August. The colours are orange and lime green with a whiff of purple from tall *Verbena bonariensis* and bulk added with the leaves of a plume poppy, *Macleaya microcarpa*. Orange, lime green and purple sounds as disgusting as a cheap ice lolly, but natural pigments have a different quality to chemical dyes. The only way you will know whether you will like it is to suck it and see. This scheme has no firm backbone of shrub or tree. It is evanescent and will not provide you with a great deal to look at for the winter, though the tall plumes of the grass *Miscanthus sinensis* 'Variegatus', included in the arrangement, will give substance until Christmas.

There are seven elements in the group, three of them doubtfully hardy. You have been warned. Penstemon, salvia and verbena are the slightly tender subjects, euphorbia, macleaya and miscanthus provide good foliage and some necessary buffering between the other plants. The annual marigold, *Calendula officinalis*, quite different from the French marigold commonly used for bedding, is the joker in the pack. It gives a lift to what would otherwise be rather a recessive colour scheme.

The sequence in which you put together the plants will depend on how much you intend to raise from seed. Perhaps the simplest way is to start with the tallest ingredient, *Verbena bonariensis*, and work down from that. Where you position the verbena will depend on the type of bed that you are planting. If it is a patch that you look at head-on, part of a border backed by a boundary fence or hedge, the verbena should go at the back, for it grows tall, 5ft/1.5m or more. If you are planting part of an island bed, then the verbena should go towards the middle, where it can erupt splendidly above the rest of the planting. The verbena needs little sideways room : it is all stem and flower. The

1 *Verbena bonariensis*

DECIDUOUS PERENNIAL
HEIGHT AND SPREAD
5 FT X 20 IN/150 X 50 CM
ZONE 8–10

Like salvia, this is a natural perennial that is perhaps safest thought of as an annual. If it overwinters you can then pride yourself on your cleverness. If it does not, it is not your fault. This verbena is an accommodating plant. Although tall, it is not demanding of sideways space. Most of the leaves are clustered in a basal rosette from which rises a tall branching stem. At the end of each branch is a tight head of tiny purple flowers which bloom continuously from June until frosts stop the show. Bracken or weathered ashes spread over the plants when they have died down will provide extra winter protection. They are reasonably easy to raise from seed. The most important thing is not to get the compost too wet. Moisten it well before sowing the seed, cover the seed thinly with dryish compost, cover the seed tray with black polythene and keep it around 70°F/20°C until the seeds have germinated. They will need pricking out, growing on and hardening off before planting.

2 *Penstemon*

SEMI-EVERGREEN PERENNIAL
HEIGHT AND SPREAD
3 X 2 FT/90 X 60 CM
ZONE 8–10

Some cultivars of this desirable group are bigger than others. 'Apple Blossom' rarely exceeds 18in/45cm in any direction. The popular 'Garnet' with narrow leaves and sprays of wine-red flowers hovers around 30in/75cm while the lilac-blue 'Alice Hindley' in a good year, particularly where it has been able to overwinter successfully, can spread

to 4ft/120cm. All are beautiful, but unfortunately not reliably hardy. Stem cuttings taken in August or early September root easily and can be overwintered with protection. Damp is as much an enemy as frost and you will please them by finding them a well-drained spot in full sun. Do not cut down stems in autumn, as new shoots will get slaughtered by frost.

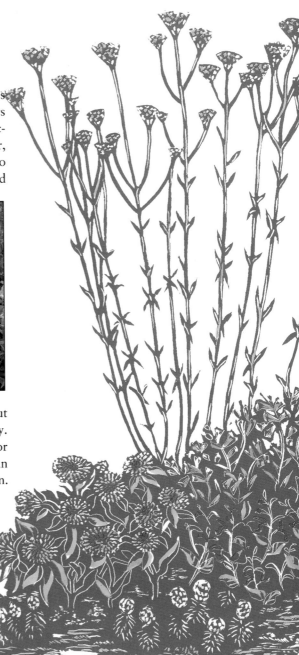

3 *Euphorbia sequieriana niciciana* (**Spurge**)

EVERGREEN PERENNIAL
HEIGHT AND SPREAD
15 X 15IN/38 X 38CM
ZONE 7–9

This is a neat member of a family in which there are some hefty giants. All the spurges have characteristically lime-coloured flowers, some more yellowish than others. Although outlandish, they fit with any colour you put against them and they are generally undemanding in their requirements. *E. sequieriana niciciana* is a low-growing spurge and throws up a mass of elegant arching stems covered with thread-like leaves, distinctly greyish in tone. These are topped with sulphurous flowers in late spring. They last well, but fade to a less arresting colour. Plants can be cut back after flowering to encourage fresh, compact growth.

4 *Salvia patens*

DECIDUOUS PERENNIAL
HEIGHT AND SPREAD
24 X 18IN/60 X 45CM
ZONE 5–10

If it is not knocked back by frost, this salvia eventually makes fleshy underground tubers rather like a dahlia's, though it is nothing like as vigorous in growth. Foliage is mid-green and the beaky flowers are piercing blue in the standard form, paler sky-coloured in the variety 'Cambridge Blue'. They are sparse and, as with most salvias, there is a greater proportion of leaf to flower than one would wish. Space of their own is vital as these plants are not fighters. They are Mexicans and need sun. They are quite easy to raise from seed. Mid-April will be early enough to

sow at a temperature around 65°F/ 18°C. Unlike verbena, salvias like a very moist compost and it must never be allowed to dry out. After pricking out, keep the plants at around 55°F/ 13°C until they can be hardened off and set out at the end of May.

5 *Calendula officinalis* (**Pot marigold**)

HARDY ANNUAL
HEIGHT AND SPREAD
24 X 15IN/60 X 38CM
ZONE 4–9

Its proper name comes from the Latin *calendae*, the first day of the month, and is a tribute to the long flowering period of this common cottage-garden flower. They are charming and easy annuals, flowering best in sun. Regular dead-heading will prolong the display. Sow seed where it is to flower, covering lightly with soil. Thin out seedlings as they develop. Powdery mildew can be a nuisance.

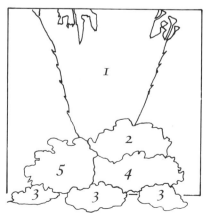

stem, exactly square in section, has pairs of small leaves at sparse intervals. From the leaf joints and at the top of the stem grow clusters of tiny flowers, a good rich mauve or pale purple. It is an excellent flowerer, particularly if you are lucky enough to have plants that have overwintered for they will then get going by the end of June and still be flowering by the end of October. You never get tired of them, for they are delicate and the colour obliging enough to fit itself in with whatever is going on round it. It needs no staking and its tall, rather gaunt habit of growth is in itself charming. Most perennials fuss about too long with their leaves before they consider tossing you a flower. This verbena gets straight on with the job. It does not even need dead-heading, as the flowers all push out in succession from the same starting point. You can buy ready grown plants from some nurseries. Beth Chatto usually has them. So does Christopher Lloyd at Great Dixter. The plants are devoted self-seeders, so once introduced, you will probably never be without. Even if your plants do not overwinter, their progeny will be sitting in the ground, ready to bounce into action in the spring. They are also reasonably easy to raise from seed yourself.

This verbena will, on its own, furnish the top layer of this group. Three plants, macleaya, miscanthus and penstemon will take care of the middle storey, though one of them will constantly be trying to topple the verbena as king of the heap. This is the plume poppy which can be a bully. It has thickly glaucous stems and handsome deeply lobed leaves, bronze green with grey undersides. Plumes of buff-coloured flowers, more of a hazy impression than a series of separately defined blooms, start opening in June and continue to the end of August. The foliage makes a strong contribution all season. This plant is a seducer. It only shows its faults when you have already fallen in love and by then it is too late to escape. This is a familiar scenario.

You will meet people who have had bad experiences with the plume poppy. It is the villain of many horror stories, of wrecked tennis courts, where tarmac heaved up under the insistent pressure of macleaya shoots, of borders that have been slaughtered with glyphosate weedkiller to curb the colonizing plume poppy in its midst. Certainly, it needs an eye kept on it, probably two eyes. Some dogs are like this though. If you wrote down all the awful things they did, you would suppose you would be put off by them, but somehow you are not. There are enough endearing characteristics to set on the credit side. Just as you can cuff a dog when it gets above itself, so the gardener must keep the plume poppy in check. It spreads by underground suckers and you have no idea in which direction these are moving until a new shoot bobs up, usually in the middle of some choice clump of something rather difficult. Then without delay you must ease this shoot out of the ground and gently pull up the runner without breaking it, until you reach back to the original legal clump, where, with a victorious thrust of the spade, you can chop it off. You could even pot the runner up with its shoot and sell it for an inflated sum in aid of needy bachelors or redundant beam engines, wherever your conscience lies. So with this proviso, plant macleaya and enjoy it.

Miscanthus will not prove such a handful. It is content to clump up slowly and gracefully from the centre out, with no underhand dealings below ground. In this family will be found some of the best of the ornamental grasses. *Miscanthus sinensis* 'Variegatus' has a broad creamy stripe down the centre of each leaf, which, when the plant is established, may be up to 4ft/120cm long. It is not leafy in the way that herbaceous perennials are, but a plant that seems to have been assembled by a sculptor, working with fine polished wire. It needs no staking and its thin leaves arch gracefully over plants without getting in their way or depriving them of light and air.

Penstemon is the second doubtfully hardy ingredient in the group. For years you may be lucky and begin to take their survival for granted. Then suddenly there is a winter that wipes out all your dreams. Penstemons are ridiculously easy to root from cuttings taken in late summer and also layer themselves enthusiastically. By either of these methods, you will be able to hedge your bets and beat the most malevolent winter frosts. The penstemons, because they bloom for the whole of the summer, with a few stray flowers still appearing at the end of October, have become hugely popular. Most are 2–3ft/60–90cm high with tubular flowers held rather in the manner of a foxglove on the upper part of the stem. Colours range from deep red through to palest pink, but a blue is what is needed in this scheme, and a fairly vigorous one such as 'Alice Hindley'. This is flushed with deeper colour on the topsides of the flower. The same colour stains the edges of the insides of the petals, which are generally paler in tone. It is a gorgeous plant and a tidy grower when it is young, though inclined to sprawl in age. In a mild winter, penstemons never lose their leaves. If foliage is cut back by frost, clean up the plant in spring when you can see what is dead and what is pretending.

The three remaining plants will furnish the bottom level of planting, but only one with any degree of permanency. This is a neat spurge, *Euphorbia sequieriana niciciana* which throws up a mass of delicate arching stems. Each is thickly clothed with fine blue-green foliage, arranged like a bottle brush. The flowers are an uncompromising sulphurous lime, magnificent with the penstemon. *Salvia patens* should be fitted in near it too, another perennial that, like verbena, is safer thought of as an annual. Many of the salvias, now so much in vogue, make a disproportionate amount of leaf to flower, but *S.*

patens has things arranged more equably. Another problem with salvias, when raised annually from seed as many of them have to be in our climate, is that their first flowering coincides suicidally with the first frosts. Here again, *S. patens* is more sensible. There are two forms. The plain named version has flowers of a piercing gentian blue. *S. patens* 'Cambridge Blue' has softer, paler flowers. Both are equally desirable and both grow about 2ft/60cm high, with rough, bright foliage. The bottom half of each flower is splayed out in a broad lip. The top half folds over on itself to enclose the stamens and bends over the lower half like a claw. The plants are never swarming with flowers. They come out in ones and twos over a long period, but always catch the eye because the colour is so intense. As plants mature, they develop swollen tubers very like a dahlia's. Some authorities recommend treating them the same way, digging them up and storing them inside during the winter. On the whole, it is probably better to leave them in the ground and take the precaution of gathering a little seed every autumn. They are quite easy to raise from seed.

The final touch in this scheme comes from marigolds, varieties of *Calendula officinalis* or the English marigold. The self-seedlings you see are generally bright orange, but for this scheme something more complex is called for. 'Pacific Apricot' has buds of deep brown-orange opening to a gentle, washed-out apricot. 'Art Shades Mixed', blended for aesthetes, has a wider range of colours – apricot, orange, cream – with dark brown button eyes. These both grow to about 2ft/60cm, but there are dwarf varieties, such as 'Fiesta Gitana Mixed', only half that height. With attention to dead-heading, marigolds will flower well. Sow later rather than earlier if you want them to peak in August. If you bring them on too early, they will have shot their bolt by July. The easiest method is to sow seed direct into the ground. If you sow around mid-April, then the marigolds should still be looking good in August. They can be martyrs to mildew. If this worries you, spray with a systemic fungicide every couple of weeks in the growing season. If cats, birds, children and other adversaries make sowing direct a difficulty, raise seeds inside in the usual way and put plants out before they have got too big.

Trimming a hydrangea

The second planting scheme for August has a hydrangea as its centrepiece, for we must acknowledge the hydrangea's position as shrub of the month. There is a beefiness about the mop-headed hydrangea that is not altogether satisfactory. This scheme uses instead tall *Hydrangea aspera villosa*, flanked by the variegated leaves of *Fuchsia magellanica* 'Versicolor'. It will demand rather more space than the first group, though the hydrangea does not swell out in the characteristic fashion of the mopheads. It grows up, to at least 6ft/1.8cm, and the side branches tend to bend down to make a narrow skirt round the main stem. The general effect is gaunt, but splendid, a narrow pyramid shape clothed with large, rough, pointed leaves, and in late summer, flowers of the lacecap type. The heads are large, with deep pink florets surrounding a group of tiny flowers in the centre : brilliant blue stamens on a pink base. You only see all this when you are nose to nose with the plant. From a distance, the impression is of rich violet.

If possible, you should arrange for the hydrangea to sit in partial shade. By nature it is a woodland plant and enjoys the kind of dappled shade that may come from the branches of tall trees nearby. If shade is not to be found, mulch the shrub thickly with leaves, muck or compost in spring to keep the roots cool and well fed. Do not cram it up against a fence, which will cramp its elegant style. It will need to be at the back of this particular group, as it is so tall, but give it room. Keep a firm grip on your secateur trigger finger too. Pruning does not hurt the hydrangea, in the sense that it will die back if cut, but it is very difficult to cut out branches without unbalancing the whole creation.

This scheme, mostly in purple, pink and blue, revolves around the hydrangea, so get this in first and then fiddle around with the other components, the variegated fuchsia and a bush of either the soft yellow argyranthemum 'Jamaica Primrose' or a blue osteospermum. These are the basics. Galtonias, white lilies and agapanthus provide the trimmings. The fuchsia will go in front of the hydrangea, but not too close. Its neat pink, cream and grey-green leaves contrast well with the rough foliage of the other. The fuchsia, though often cut down to the base each year by winter frosts, never fails to make up lost ground by July. The flowers are not so dramatic as the more highly bred fuchsias. They are long, narrow, deep red with purple tubes, just the sort of flowers you see on fuchsia hedges in the West Country or in south-west Ireland. They can be counted as extras. In a hot summer they equal the foliage in value, but often the leaves give more for your money than the flowers. The new growths are very heavily flushed with pink, which subsides to a gentle grey-green as the leaves age. Occasionally growths revert to plain green. Cut these out immediately, before the whole bush begins to think that this is a good idea.

The hydrangea must have first call on any shade that is available. Fuchsia will do its best in either sun or half shade, but it cannot be expected to look good in a very murky, overhung hole. In shade the growth will tend to be more lax and the flowers fewer. The third addition, whether it be argyranthemum or osteospermum needs sun, as much as you can arrange. Both are tender and both need some special attention to

1 *Hydrangea aspera villosa*

DECIDUOUS SHRUB
HEIGHT AND SPREAD
6 X 6 FT/1.8 X 1.8 M
ZONE 7–9

Shade is the prime necessity for this superb shrub, not necessarily full, but certainly dappled. It does best in rich, deep, moist leaf-mould in light woodland, but light woodland is not always to hand in the average garden. Keep its roots cool with regular, liberal mulches in spring and try to keep it out of the full blast of the prevailing

wind, which may scorch the fine foliage. Flowers are of the lacecap type: round, flat clusters with the insignificant pink-blue flowers surrounded by showy sterile bracts of an elegant mauve. The shrub was introduced by E. H. Wilson from western Sichuan, China, in 1908 and has the advantage of being as happy on lime as on acid soils. Regular pruning is not necessary, but one-third of old growths can be cut out in rotation each spring to encourage large leaves and flower heads. The lowest branches will layer themselves naturally, given the chance. Otherwise propagate from non-flowering shoots in August or September.

2 *Fuchsia magellanica* 'Versicolor'

DECIDUOUS SHRUB
HEIGHT AND SPREAD
4 X 5 FT/1.2 X 1.5 M
ZONE 7–9

This is what is loosely called a hardy fuchsia, but it is only hardy in relation to the frilly varieties that never leave the protection of their pots. In a tough winter it may get cut down to the ground, but is unlikely to be killed outright. No regular pruning is needed. Cut out any growth that reverts to plain green and cut out (in late spring) dead branches that show no signs of breaking into bud. Any well-drained soil, alkaline or acid, will suit it, in sun or part-shade.

3 *Argyranthemum*
(Marguerite)
EVERGREEN PERENNIAL
HEIGHT AND SPREAD
3 X 3 FT/90 X 90 CM
ZONE 9–10

This is the new name for *Chrysanthemum frutescens* and it is hardly an improvement. The common marguerite or Paris daisy has white flowers like our wild moon daisy and is often used in tubs in town gardens. 'Jamaica Primrose' is a fine, pale, soft yellow form, very free-flowering, though, like all this family, not hardy. In a sheltered spot and in a mild winter, they may survive. Replace plants annually or take stem cuttings in early autumn. The flowers are long-lasting and regular dead-heading prolongs the performance – sometimes a six-month run.

4 *Galtonia candicans*
BULB
HEIGHT AND SPREAD
48 X 8 IN/120 X 120 CM
ZONE 7–10

This is a native of the eastern Cape, where it gets rain in summer and lies dormant in winter. It will prove reliably hardy in the southern half of the country. Elsewhere it can be lifted and stored each season. Plant the bulbs any time between February and April, setting them at least 6in/15cm deep. Cut down the flowered stems in autumn. They are slow to increase, but ground well enriched with rotted compost will help them on their way.

5 *Agapanthus*
DECIDUOUS PERENNIAL
HEIGHT AND SPREAD
36 X 18 IN/90 X 45 CM
ZONE 8–9

This South African needs a warm, sunny site if it is to flower well and soil that does not dry out, yet drains well in winter. *A. campanulatus* and its various forms together with the 'Headbourne Hybrids', bred in a garden at Headbourne Worthy, near Winchester, are the hardiest types available. Even these plants cannot be depended upon to come through very cold winters. The most tender are those with broad, evergreen leaves, only worth risking outside in the mild southwest of the country. Some winter protection – leaves, ashes, fern fronds – will be a useful insurance policy. Several different shades of blue are available as well as a creamy white. If you are fussy about the exact shade, buy plants in containers at flowering time, when you can see exactly how they will perform. Plant them in April, setting the crowns about 2in/5cm deep.

bring them through the winter. Alternatively you could view their impermanence as an asset and, if they curl up their toes, replace with a different member of their tribe, perhaps the pale pink argyranthemum 'Mary Wootton' or the dotty osteospermum with pinched petals called 'Whirligig'. Some gardeners take it as a personal insult if plants die on them, but if we persist in growing these exotics from the Canary Islands and South Africa, we cannot expect them to adapt instantly to our grisly winters. A couple of million years of evolution might do the trick.

The argyranthemums (formerly *Chrysanthemum frutescens* or marguerites) have recently exploded on the summer garden scene. They are evergreen (if given the chance), woody, bushy perennials with good, deeply divided green leaves, that over a full growing season will make a bush about 3ft/90cm high and wide. The form is always shapely. Some forms are more eager to flower than others. 'Jamaica Primrose' is ludicrously extravagant, pushing up wave after wave of blooms held above the ferny leaves. If a plant has overwintered, it may be in bloom by the end of May and still going strong by the end of October. If you have set out a new plant or an overwintered cutting at the end of May, then you will have to wait longer for it to get into its stride. 'Jamaica Primrose' has soft yellow daisy flowers, the petals slightly paler on the underside than they are on top, each with a bright yellow button eye. The stems are strong and wiry and the flowers last as well when picked as they do growing on the bush.

Osteospermums, which used to be dimorphothecas (botanists, like Lewis Carroll's children, do it 'to annoy, because they know it teases') are similarly tender. Varieties such as 'Cannington Roy' form low mats of foliage, evergreen if the winter allows, with large pink daisy flowers, each with a dark eye, floating around on top. The foliage is not as good as the argyranthemum's, but both have charm. *Osteospermum* 'Whirligig' has bluish-white flowers, with dark blue centres, but its chief attraction is the form of the flowers. Each petal is pinched together for half its length and then opens out at the end to make a spoon shape. It is mad, but carefree rather than painfully so.

Now the extras : tall galtonias, some outrageous white lily such as the Japanese *L. auratum* and, if you live in the pampered south, clumps of agapanthus. Galtonias, summer hyacinths, grow about 3ft/90cm tall, with strong stems carrying up to thirty fleshy white bell flowers, slightly tinged with green. They are not too leafy – a great advantage in mixed planting schemes. One bulb might be missed if you blink at the wrong time. Plant five reasonably close together for the best effect.

Agapanthus look as though they should be bulbs too, for they have the fleshy leaves that one associates with hyacinths and the like, and belong to the same family as lilies.

They have strappy foliage, like the galtonias, shorter, but usually more of it. Like the galtonia, too, they cannot be considered hardy in cold areas of the country. Some hybrids are tougher than others. The flowers are blue (white in the form 'Alice Gloucester') and borne in big round umbels on stout 3ft/90cm stems. Agapanthus ramble like weeds over the sand dunes at Tresco in the Scilly Isles, where they were once grown commercially as cut flowers. They do not always flower so profusely away from the balmy south-west. 'Headbourne Hybrids' are looked on as being relatively tough, also 'Dorothy Palmer', with flowers of rich blue. The narrower the leaf, the hardier the type will prove.

The lilies can be planted in spring as it is almost impossible to get hold of them at the prime moving time in late September and October. The difficulty in spring is that bulbs may be excessively dry and shrivelled. Unlike other bulbs such as daffodils, they have no outer protective coat. You must buy them before they start sprouting. In garden centres you sometimes see lily bulbs pushing out shoots among the wood shavings in a desperate attempt to keep to the timetable that nature devised, rather than that of some godforsaken marketing department. These bulbs are not good buys. A plant needs to concentrate on one thing at a time : roots first, shoots after, when they can be sustained by the roots. Shoots springing from dry bulbs are living on capital and there is no future in that.

The white *L. auratum* is not difficult to grow, but is short-lived. It will do best in a relatively lime-free soil with its feet in the shade and its head in the sun. It is stem-rooting, so needs to be planted deep. Where it is happy, it will zoom up to 6ft/1.8m or more with heads of exotic flowers, at least 6in/15cm across, sometimes twice as much as that. It is expensive, relative to other lily bulbs, but well worth it for the smell alone.

SEPTEMBER

IN TEMPERAMENT, SEPTEMBER IS ON THE CUSP OF THE YEAR. IT WILL depend partly on where you live, partly on your personality whether you regard the month as the end of summer or the beginning of autumn. North of the Wash, it will feel decidedly autumnal. There may be early morning frosts, particularly in valley bottoms, which, though no more than an early warning of what is to come, may still be enough to stop quintessentially summer flowers such as geraniums in their tracks and perhaps blacken the foliage of dahlias before they have fully got into their stride. In the south, September may quietly drift by in a long sequence of warm, still, lusciously overblown days with more sun than ever appeared between June and August. Yet there is an undercurrent of warning : the early mornings have a particular coolness, the dews are heavy. The sun is lower in the sky and the shadows consequently longer across one's garden. There is a particular smell about September too, that marks it indelibly : the sharp, pungent, slightly acid aroma of Michaelmas daisies and the sweet, senescent smell of the first windfalls, left to rot in long grass.

Although there is often a month of good growing weather ahead, September too often staggers by on a diet of leftovers from the plantings of previous months : ragged acanthus, the fag-ends of crocosmia, gently mildewing annuals. There is a reluctance on the part of the gardener to put too much effort into September, feeling, like an apocalyptic preacher, that the end is nigh. Thirty days is a long time to waste, however, and there are plenty of plants, particularly those growing from bulbs and corms, which make their debut now : cyclamen, nerines, colchicums, belladonna lilies, autumn crocus in soft shades of purple and pink, sternbergias in blazing buttercup yellow.

There is a fine freshness about these exiles from hotter lands. All of them effortlessly revitalize the garden scene, changing the tedium of over-familiarity into unexpected novelty. Autumn bulbs have never found their way into the gardening calendar in the way that spring ones have. Even kindergarten gardeners know that daffodils must be planted in autumn to flower in spring. Most spring-flowering bulbs – crocus, tulips, grape hyacinths – adapt to the same simple timetable. Autumn flowering bulbs are not so easy to categorize and have more complicated growing patterns. Most come from areas where they lie dormant and baked through a hot summer to be tickled into bloom by the first rains of autumn. The belladonna from South Africa follows this life cycle, so does the sternbergia from the Mediterranean. Colchicum and autumn crocus split their growth between autumn and spring : flowers in one season, leaves in another. Cyclamen also flower before they start to think about leaves, but get the two acts running concurrently so that leaves appear towards the end of September, together with the last of the flowers. The foliage, handsomely marked with silver, then remains to furnish the garden through winter and spring. These different habits of growth affect planting times. Cyclamen and colchicums need to be snatched some time during August, as soon as they appear in shops and garden centres, and planted immediately. Colchicums will usually bloom as soon as their feet hit base, sometimes before. Cyclamen often need a season to settle before they swing into action, but once established, are among the most undemanding of plants. They will also grow in unpropitious places, in shade or among the roots of the shrub that will provide the centrepiece of your autumn planting scheme. Belladonnas are usually sold in spring and are only likely to succeed in a hot, sunny position where the bulbs can get well baked in summer. Nerines, also from South Africa might appear in bulb catalogues in either autumn or spring and need the same sort of growing conditions as belladonnas. This confusion about when autumn-flowering bulbs are available and when they should be planted may perhaps be the reason why, as a group, they have never been as widely planted as spring bulbs. They are all, by nature, bottom-tier plants, but will give pleasure out of all proportion to their size.

September is also the season for spiky exotics such as yucca from the southern United States and the phormiums or New Zealand flaxes. These are not to everybody's taste. They are determinedly foreign, harsh, though arresting, in form and sometimes difficult to fit in with the soft, hummocky, gently foliaged plants usually seen in English gardens. The sculptural forms of phormium and their like fit well into heavily architectural gardens. They also look excellent in small town gardens, with paving, pools and pergolas, but less good perhaps in a country setting where the background may be of native trees, hedges, green fields. Gertrude Jekyll used yucca in mixed plantings, notably in her main flower border at Munstead Wood, where with bergenia it provided solid anchors of foliage at either end of her scheme.

Either yucca or phormium could be used as the centrepiece for a September planting scheme of purple, pink and white to hold autumn at bay. Both these plants need a little space around them, so their striking symmetrical form is not muddled by neighbours' flopping growth. *Yucca gloriosa* 'Variegata' has a dense rosette of leaves, margined and striped with a pale creamy yellow. They are as stiff as swords and as pointed. This is not a comfortable plant, but it is dramatic, even without the flowers, which come in dense cream spires in September. *Y. filamentosa* flowers earlier and younger, at about three years old. Do not bother with either unless you can give them well-drained ground and full sun. Sandy soils are ideal. Groups of Japanese anemones, either white or pink, can be used with the yucca, though not too close. These are endlessly forgiving plants, which thrive in the mangiest positions that a sadistic gardener can devise. If planted with the yucca, they will have full sun, for that is what the yucca demands, but they will also flower in deep shade and in a wide variety of soils. They do not need staking, though the flowers are borne on 4ft/120cm high stems, well above the ruff of foliage. 'Queen Charlotte' is a reliable single pink, 'Géante des Blanches' a large-flowered vigorous white.

If the yucca has been used as the focal point of a small island bed, the anemones can grow in corresponding clumps around it, though not too symmetrically arranged. If the planting is being done in a section of border backed by a wall or hedge, then the anemones can go behind and slightly to the side of the yucca.

Sedums are also invaluable September plants. The most generous and most showy is *Sedum* 'Autumn Joy' which from a succulent base of pale green leaves produces wide, stiff flat heads of deep pink flowers. They darken as they age but keep their shape well into the winter. Young plants are usually no trouble, but as the clumps increase in size, they tend to splay out so that you gaze, not at a haze of delicious pink, but into an untidy bald hole. There are two ways to solve this irritating problem. You can dig up your clump, split it and replant a small section of the original. March or early April is the best time for this operation. If you do not want to reduce the size of the plant you will have to stake it. Surround it with a stockade of short sticks early in the season, before it has begun to flop, and wind round plenty of soft green twine so that the sedum grows up inside a reasonably firm, restraining corset. If space is at a premium, you may choose *Sedum* 'Ruby Glow' which makes a lax rosette of stems, floppy by nature, so there is no point in trying to stand them up as with 'Autumn Joy'. 'Ruby Glow' has the same succulent foliage, but it is washed over with grey-purple and the clusters of purplish-red flowers are smaller in every way than those of *S.* 'Autumn Joy'.

Michaelmas daisies are another classic ingredient in the September mix. The tribe is often a martyr to mildew, but the variety *Aster x frikartii* 'Monch' is less prone to attack than the normal *A. novi-belgii* kinds. Although at the beginning of the season their growth seems quite sparse, the stems branch well and carry large flowers, lilac-coloured with bright yellow centres. It needs discreet support. Small pieces of twiggy stick pushed in as the plant is getting going in midsummer are probably the easiest. *Aster lateriflorus* 'Horizontalis' does not need staking. It is a stubby, self-contained Michaelmas daisy with flowers that individually make less impact than an ant on a satellite dish, but massed together give a very pleasing gentle grey-pink haze. If you do get close to look, you see that most of the colour comes from the dusty pink central boss. The petals are tiny, sparse and white. As the season wears on, the foliage is sometimes flushed with purple – an extremely pleasing combination. Altogether this is a subtle plant and quite slow to increase. You will probably need to plant three together in a clump to get the right effect. It is said to need full sun, but flowers perfectly adequately in dappled – though not overhung – shade. If you are tinkering with the thought of a michaelmas daisy to use in the foreground of a September planting scheme, *A. divaricatus* is probably the answer. It has thin, wiry, nearly black stems and rather sparse but starry white flowers. In its wildish way, it is very appealing, but it is a loller. It looks as uncomfortable as a person jacked up in a neck brace if you try and stake it. It is anyway only two feet tall and so does not loll too destructively. The flowers last well and the foliage is cleaner, greener and less prone to mildew than the showier, true michaelmas daisies, varieties of *A. novi-belgii*.

Nerines, which zoom leafless out of the ground this month, need the benefit of all the sun that shines and so are natural companions for plants such as the yucca, which also needs full sun. They explode in soft umbels of pink flowers held on top of bare 18in/45cm stems. The chief problem lies in getting them to flower regularly. The bulbs are about the same size as daffodil and should be planted so that the neck is level with the surface of the soil. A good head will have as many as nine blooms, each with six long strappy petals that curl back on themselves to reveal purple stamens. *Nerine bowdenii* is the only species with any claim to hardiness. 'Fenwick's Variety' is the type to get hold of if you can. It is a particularly robust form, larger and more vigorous than the species, with deeper pink flowers. The flowers often continue well until November and are then followed by the leaves, which overwinter and die down the following summer. One on its own looks as lively as a left-behind swallow. Plant in groups of at least half a dozen, leaving roughly 6in/15cm between each bulb. They do not like being disturbed, so will not suit restless gardeners who are forever worrying their plants. It is not fully hardy and needs a light sandy soil to give its best. Heavy clay soils should be leavened with a mixture of coarse sand and leaf-mould. Varieties such as 'Orion' and 'Brian Doe' are even less hardy than the species and are most likely to succeed in a bulb frame or cool greenhouse.

Neat shrubs

If you feel nervous about inviting yucca or any of its spiky friends into the garden, you can construct a more traditional plant group using the neat small shrubs caryopteris and abelia as anchors, with phlox and asters as extras to add bulk. If there is some dappled shade, cyclamen could be used in the foreground to take care of the bottom level of planting. This collection is in soft blue, mauve and pink. If you want a sunnier scene to warm the garden before autumn takes a hold, turn straight to pages 120–121 for a scheme in brilliant yellow and blue. Colour scheming in the garden causes an inordinate amount of worry. Using a good proportion of foliage to flowers is one way to buffer the effect of using strongly contrasting colours. Yellow is often singled out as the villain in 'spoiling' colour schemes, but it would be a sad garden that never saw any yellow. Sugar-almond pink is the only colour with which it sometimes quarrels. Keep those two apart and you will find that few other combinations cause problems, unless you are extremely finely tuned. If this is the case, only green flowers will suffice.

There is little to be frightened of in the caryopteris scheme. All the plants in the group are neat and compact and you can drop one or other of the shrubby components, caryopteris or abelia, and leave out the asters altogether, if you are trying to fit your September planting into a very small space. We often go overboard with plants that perform during the first half of the season, leaving insufficient room for those that peak from August to October. This is one way to redress the balance.

Caryopteris x clandonensis is a grey-leaved shrub, more truthfully grey-green, that, after a severe cutting back in March, produces new wands of growth. In the axils of the paired leaves, small fluffy clusters of smoky-blue flowers bloom during August and September. It is compact, seldom more than 4ft/120cm in any direction, and the effect of the whole exactly in tune with September's mood, when the light is low and more diffuse than in high summer and the morning colours fractured by heavy dews. The shrub has a natural, well-balanced grace and is not fussy about soil. It does need sun to flower well and may need winter protection in cold, exposed gardens. 'Arthur Simmonds' is a good variety, hardier than other types. So is the slightly more upright 'Heavenly Blue'. 'Kew Blue' has more telling flowers, a richer, deeper shade of blue.

With, or instead of the caryopteris, use *Abelia x grandiflora*, as neat and arching a plant as the former, but not very good at fighting for *Lebensraum*. It needs the help of a dictator to keep more opportunistic plants at bay. Given time, it may heave itself up as high as 6ft/1.8m, but for years may hang around content to view life at the caryopteris's level. It has bright green shiny leaves, neat and pointed, a good contrast with the caryopteris's pale, matt-textured foliage. The flowers are white with the faintest flush of pink, but because they emerge from prominent copper-pink calyces, the general colour effect of the shrub in full bloom is warm pink. It is semi-evergreen, which is an advantage, and needs little pruning. Dead wood can be cut out in spring and old wood taken out after flowering, if you feel the thing is getting too big for its boots. This is a good shrub, but quiet, so that you take it for granted. 'Francis Mason' is the variety to look for.

To beef up this restrained pair, use clumps of the fine variegated phlox 'Norah Leigh'. This has such good foliage – cream and green with the newest leaves almost entirely cream – that it scarcely needs its rather wishy-washy flowers of lilac, just coming out now. Phlox are great trenchermen and to get the best results from them, you need to mulch them well with compost or well-rotted muck in early spring. They also need to be reinvigorated by regular splitting and replanting when clumps become congested. They will not need staking, which is a great benefit. Since you will be growing 'Norah Leigh' rather more for its foliage than for its flowers, you will not have to thin out the flowering stems, which is the usual cultural practice where you want flower heads of maximum size.

If there is room, add some plants of an annual aster between the shrubs and the phlox. This will require forethought, for you either have to buy small plants in spring, or raise them yourself from seed. The second alternative is the better if you have the space and are not daunted by the process. The purveyors of bedding plants rarely grow the more interesting members of any particular family. The aster colours, predominantly pink and mauve with an occasional leavening of creamy-white, consort well with both caryopteris and abelia.

Wilt is their worst enemy and it is untreatable. Spores linger in the soil for years and there is no way of knowing whether they are there until your plants suddenly and dramatically collapse. Better not to think about it, for it would be a pity not to grow them at all. Height is the chief consideration in choosing varieties. 'Giant Florett' will reach 30in/75cm and has enormous flowers packed with thin, quilled petals, each backed with a ruff of green. The blooms are so full that you get no glimpse of the central yellow disc that is so prominent in other varieties such as 'Giant Single Andrella'. 'Pinocchio' is much more dwarf, only 8in/20cm high. The plants make a compact mound smothered

1 *Caryopteris x clandonensis*

DECIDUOUS SHRUB
HEIGHT AND SPREAD
3 X 3 FT/90 X 90 CM
ZONE 7–9

Neat, well-balanced, fast-growing shrub with pointed grey-green leaves that, when crushed, have an aromatic tang, similar to lavender. Clusters of pale blue flowers appear in the leaf axils during August and September. 'Heavenly Blue' has mid-blue flowers and generally makes a smaller, more compact shrub than the type. They need cutting back hard each March. Flowers are produced on the new growth made each season. All like full sun and a light, well-drained soil.

2 Abelia x grandiflora

SEMI-EVERGREEN SHRUB
HEIGHT AND SPREAD
6 X 4 FT/1.8 X 1.2 M
ZONE 8–10

Vigorous arching shrub with small, glossy, pointed leaves. Pink and white tubular flowers are borne from July to October and are lightly scented. The shrub is named after Clarke Abel, the eighteenth century doctor who introduced it. There are several different varieties. 'Francis Mason' is one of the best known. The foliage is washed with golden yellow, but it is not the best choice for cold parts of the country as it is slightly more tender than its parent. It will succeed in any soil, but flowers most freely in full sun. No regular pruning is needed, but you can thin out overcrowded or unshapely growths after flowering. Propagate by semi-ripe cuttings taken in July which should be ready for planting out in spring.

3 Phlox paniculata

DECIDUOUS PERENNIAL
HEIGHT AND SPREAD
36 X 18 IN/90 X 45 CM
ZONE 6–9

The herbaceous phloxes are an enormous family, but few are grown for their foliage, the chief asset of the variety 'Norah Leigh'. The leaves more than make up for the pusillanimous flowers. 'Harlequin' has a stronger constitution, but is less strikingly variegated than 'Norah Leigh'. Deep, moist, well-fed soils will give the best results, in sun or light shade. Cut flowering stems to the ground in early winter and mulch with some organic material in spring.

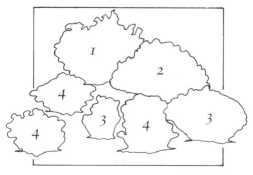

4 Aster

HALF-HARDY ANNUAL
HEIGHT AND SPREAD
Varies widely
ZONE 5–9

The annual aster (properly *Callistephus* or China aster) is a charming addition to a late summer display. They are relatively slow to develop from seed. Wilt may be a problem if you always grow them in the same place. There are many different forms available, single or double, with petals that are flat or quilled, curved inwards like a chrysanthemum or flailing in all directions like some frenetic mop. Height varies from 24in/60cm ('Giant Princess', 'Giant Florett') to a dwarf 8in/20cm ('Pinocchio Mixed', 'Milady Mixed'). Seed can be sown inside in trays of moist compost during late March or April at a temperature of 65°F/18°C. This is a more reliable method than direct sowing outside in April or May. Prick out the seedlings when they have developed their first proper leaves and plant them outside towards the end of May. Stake taller varieties.

with small double flowers in the usual aster colours. 'Ostrich Plume' is an old favourite, intermediate in height (18in/45cm) with marvellous great shaggy flower heads. The plants branch well from the base and the variety has good resistance to the dreaded wilt.

If the conditions are suitable, you could use the autumn-flowering cyclamen *C. hederifolium* instead. It is important to give this the right position. It would be lost near the asters, which will crush it through sheer force of personality, like some great blowsy bar singer embracing a reclusive poet. If you use the tall asters, they can be placed in open ground back from the border's edge, but the ground under the arching branches of the caryopteris will be better for the little cyclamen. If you cannot fit them in here use them instead on their own under a tree in the dry ground where few other things will grow. There is no garden, however small, that cannot find room for a few corms. Of all the plants in this season, this is the one that you should not be without. Cyclamen do not shout at you. They are gentle plants, but it is odd how, once you have got them in the garden, you find endless excuses to go and see how they are doing. Part of their charm is that they are always doing well. If you are extremely short-sighted, their delights will be blurred, for they do not venture more than four inches off the ground. Like fingerprints, no two leaves are the same, but they all have the innate ability to hold themselves well and to arrange themselves thoughtfully in the clump, so that all have equal opportunity to display their intricate paintwork.

Nothing looks more unlikely to produce flowers than these wizened discs of dried dung, but once you have sorted out which way up to plant them (vestigial remains are more likely to be shoots than roots and should go uppermost) nothing is more trouble-free. The flowers, various shades of pale pink or, in the form *album*, pure white, have the typical swept-back heads of the cyclamen family. They are enchanting things, as fragile as porcelain to look at, although the corms from which they spring are themselves as tough and as well equipped for survival as the most macho commando. Corms should be barely covered with soil. Bonemeal and a mulch of leaf-mould in the summer when the leaves die down is all the sustenance that they ask. The leaves appear with the last of the flowers and are as great an asset. They are roughly ivy-shaped and marbled with silver on a dark green background, each leaf with a different pattern. They persist until May. In the past vast quantities of cyclamen corms have been brought into this country from Turkey, but wild stocks are becoming seriously depleted. Corms dug from the wild may be so desiccated by the time they reach the customer that they can never be resuscitated. If you do not know anyone whom you might persuade to part with a few corms, try if possible to buy corms grown in this country. They can be planted from pots at any time of the year. Old corms reach an enormous size, as big as a dinner plate, and produce perhaps a hundred flowers. The seed-pods are extraordinary, like punch balls on springs, lying flat on the ground. Ants busily disperse the seed, but you can beat them to it if you want to enlarge your colony (and you will). Sow the seed as soon as you have collected it and nurse the plantlets along until they have several leaves and can fend for themselves in the garden jungle.

In praise of yellow

The final planting scheme for September has been put together in honour of a relatively little used bulb, *Sternbergia lutea*, which has splendid brilliant yellow flowers, rather larger than – but akin to – the crocus. It is actually a member of the amaryllis family and is named after an eighteenth-century Austrian botanist, Count Kaspar von Sternberg. It is a Mediterranean bulb, but puts up perfectly happily with our drabber climate. It will flower best in the same warm, sunny spot that nerines prefer. It is fashionable to be snooty about yellow flowers – except of course those *divine* sulphurous achilleas that bloom in July and the *extraordinary* pale gladiolus *G. tristis* that come out at the same time. This is a pity. Yellow is a cheerful colour to have about, particularly now as the light becomes less intense and scraps of mist hang around softening the perception of colour. Yellow shines out, proclaiming a defiant last fling, a call to a party before everything shuts down for the winter. It would be dreary if September came and went represented only by a whimper of mauve.

Yellow and blue provide a spanking contrast when used together and the low shrub ceratostigma, with brilliant blue flowers, obligingly performs at the same time as the sternbergia. Combine them with kirengeshoma and liriope. If you have a wall or fence to spare at the back of this planting, you could add untidy swags of the late-flowering yellow *Clematis tangutica*. *Ceratostigma willmottianum* is an open floppy sort of shrub rather lacking in bulk. It may be best to cheat and plant three close together if you wish to carry out this scheme. One alone looks very thin. The flowers are an intense pure blue, without a hint of mauve. They are much more startling than those of the misty caryopteris and appear in clusters at the ends of the lax stems. A cluster, during its life, might produce thirty or more flowers, but no more than three or four of these will be out at the same time. As the weather gets colder, some leaves turn scarlet and this is glorious to see. Unlike caryopteris, it needs no regular pruning, but dead wood can be cut out in spring. It is very happy leaning out of the front of a sunny raised bed, or over a low retaining wall, if it happens that you can arrange things this way.

1 · *Sternbergia lutea*

BULB
HEIGHT AND SPREAD
5 X 5 IN/12.5 X 12.5 CM
ZONE 7–9

Find a hot, sunny spot for this Mediterranean flower, preferably one where the soil dries out to a certain extent during the summer. A mental notice 'Do Not Disturb' should be hung above this species. Plant 4–6in/ 10–15cm deep as soon as you can get hold of the bulbs in August, incorporating some bonemeal in the planting soil. Divide the clumps (in August) only when they show, by flowering less freely, that they have become overcrowded. Leave the foliage to die down naturally. The sternbergias look like crocuses, but are actually members of the amaryllis family. Brilliant golden yellow goblet flowers are set off by dark green leaves that sometimes arrive with, sometimes after the flowers.

2 Ceratostigma willmottianum

DECIDUOUS SHRUB
HEIGHT AND SPREAD
3 X 3 FT/90 X 90 CM
ZONE 7–9

Sun and well-drained soil will persuade this shrub to give of its best. The foliage is neat, rather than showy. Brilliant blue flowers are borne over a long period in late summer. Sometimes the leaves turn yellow before they fall. Growth is spindly. Plant two or three specimens together. It is reasonably hardy and it is most likely to be affected by cold before it is fully established. No regular pruning is needed, but dead or damaged growths should be cut out in March. Propagate in July, with 3in/7.5cm long cuttings of half-ripe shoots, taken off with a heel.

3 Kirengeshoma palmata

DECIDUOUS PERENNIAL
HEIGHT AND SPREAD
3 X 2 FT/90 X 60 CM
ZONE 6–9

Handsome foliage is this perennial's great asset, worth at least as much as the late flowers. Heavy clusters of buds reveal thin shuttlecock flowers about 2in/5cm long in pale creamy yellow. It will thrive in cool, humus-rich, lime-free soil in semi-shade. Cut down the stems when the foliage has died down and mulch with some nitrogenous mix in spring. Increase stock by dividing in autumn or spring.

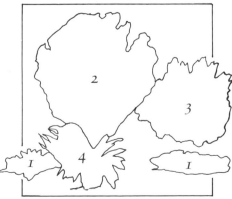

4 Liriope

EVERGREEN PERENNIAL
HEIGHT AND SPREAD
12 X 18 IN/30 X 45 CM
ZONE 7–9

Romantically named after a nymph of the fountains and mother of Narcissus, this is a most useful ground-covering plant, seen to great advantage at Kew Gardens where it makes great sheets of autumn colour. The grassy leaves make dense cover earning it its American name of lily turf. There are perhaps half a dozen different species but only two are generally available. *L. muscari*, the most common, has broad, grassy foliage of a deep shiny green and spikes of soft purple flowers, each a minuscule round bead. *L. spicata* is broadly similar, but the leaves are narrower and more erect. Both grow from swollen, fleshy rhizomes. Sun and well-drained soil will suit them well, though they will grow in partial shade. They are extremely resistant to drought. Cut out the flowering spikes when the colour has gone, but do not cut back the foliage.

The sternbergia will also want sun if it is to flower adequately and should be planted so that its companions do not flop over it while it is dormant through the summer. It is the hot summer baking that initiates flower buds in the bulb. The yellow of sternbergia is as uncompromising as the ceratostigma blue and the goblet-shaped flowers, about 2in/5cm high, are carried on leafless stems. The vigorous, strappy leaves are a pleasing dark green, an excellent foil for the flowers. If the soil is dry when you plant them (they are usually available at the end of the summer) water them well and then leave them alone. They do not like to be chivvied. If they are happy, they will clump up rapidly.

If you notice a diminution in their flower power, lift the whole clump in late spring, while the leaves are still green, and gently prise it apart into several different sections. Before you replant, refresh the soil with bonemeal or old bonfire ash, if there is any about. The remnants of potash in this are good for all flowering plants. If you know that the clump is not congested but is still not flowering, try a light dressing of potash in autumn and again in early spring, which may encourage flowers the following autumn. There is a lot of 'may' and 'might' in gardening. So much depends on the tricks of particular seasons and triggers of which we may be unaware. Be patient. It is no good storming in with your jackboots after a single season and harrying plants from pillar to post. Watch your plants, visit them as often as you can, try and decipher what they are trying to tell you. If, for instance, after the potash treatment, the sternbergia is still shy to flower, it is probably signalling, desperately, 'Take me away from here'. If you cannot provide another home, pass the bulbs on to someone who can.

The sternbergia will be sitting well to the fore of this planting scheme, clear of overhanging foliage that may provide unwelcome shade. The kirengeshoma, a fine leafy plant that will give bulk to the scheme, can go towards the back, behind the ceratostigma, or to the side of it. The leaves, rounded and lobed like a maple's, will be an asset all season. The plant grows in a strong, upright manner with wiry black stems. The flowers appear in September, funnel-shaped and of a thick, heavy texture. This is a classy plant that you do not see very often. There is usually a good reason for plants not being grown as widely as you would have thought. Kirengeshoma needs a soil very rich in humus if it is to flourish. One on the acid side of neutral will suit it perfectly. It needs shelter from wind, which could tear the fine foliage to pieces, and a modicum of dappled shade. Once you have seen it, you will think these requirements a small price to pay for the honour of having it coming to stay. Rebuild the garden if necessary as some landowners used to if a visit from Queen Victoria was on the cards.

Having exhausted yourself kowtowing to kirengeshoma's aristocratic demands, you can relax with the liriope, which is extremely undemanding. It is a perennial that looks as though it ought to be a bulb, for it grows like a grape hyacinth, less leafy, but with similar spikes of flowers in a soft shade of violet. The flowers actually look like tiny berries, round and shiny. When they first appear, you assume these must be buds which will open out into something more flower-like, but they never change. They last an exceedingly long time and the plant is useful, neat and easy to grow. It never gets above 12in/30cm high and so can be tucked in round the front of shrubs and other perennials.

The yellow clematis, which could be *C. tangutica*, is the optional extra in this group as it will need some support. From the gardener's point of view, there seems little to distinguish one from the other, but there is a variety called 'Bill Mackenzie' that has larger flowers than the type and is more vigorous. It is well worth hunting down. It is named after a curator of the Chelsea Physic Garden. Both kinds have fine fluffy seed-heads, though *cognoscenti* insist that those of *C. tangutica* have the edge over the other. The general advice is to prune hard in early spring, as you would other larger-flowering clematis. They will thrive perfectly happily unpruned, as they do in the wild and treated thus, will come into flower earlier, often by July. By September the new flowers are joined by the seed-heads of the old and the effect is charming. This is not a clematis that will easily be confined to a small space, though of course it will be more manageable if you do cut it down annually.

OCTOBER

OCTOBER IS THE TIME OF YEAR WHEN INEFFICIENTLY BRAINWASHED poetasters grope about trying to remember whatever it was that came after the 'mellow fruitfulness' bit. Autumn evidently came earlier in Keats's day. It is the month for Nature's great conjuring trick when, with splendid sleight of hand, green leaves become crimson, gold, russet and purple. Unfortunately, nobody tells you when the show is going to take place. It might come all of a rush and finish before you have had time to take in the full performance. It could be put off until November. It could be cancelled altogether. If it does happen, the leaf trick is October's grandest effect though nobody is quite sure exactly what conditions are needed for success.

It is commonly supposed that trees and shrubs colour better on acid soils than they do on alkaline ones, but at Westonbirt Arboretum in Gloucestershire, noted as the best place in England for colour in autumn, they do not find this so. At one site where there is usually a brilliant display, the soil is pH8, quite determinedly on the alkaline side of neutral (pH7). The best autumn colour often comes after the worst summers. There is a pleasing sense of justice about this, but the effect has more to do with rates of growth than fair play. In the drought years of 1976 and 1989, many trees were stressed by the shortage of water. Their natural reaction in these circumstances is to shed leaves, to cut maintenance back to the essential frame, and this may happen during August or at the beginning of September, long before the changes in temperature which generally trigger leaf fall. If they do shed leaves because of drought, trees do not bother with all the razzmatazz of colouring them beforehand. Foliage just curls up on the tree. The best effects usually happen after damp summers, when growth has been lush and unchecked. There are other factors to take into account. Gales in September can tear off leaves before the display begins. A warm, still Indian summer is what is needed, terminated by a short, sharp frost. These conditions do not come to order. All we can do is to plant a few shrubs or trees with the potential for autumn colour, then wait and hope.

Although acid soil in itself does not necessarily benefit leaf colour, several of the shrubs and trees that colour most vividly in autumn – enkianthus, fothergilla, nyssa, stewartia – are lime-haters and will only grow on acid soils. Indirectly, then, acid soil is a benefit. The maples are happy on a wide range of soils and from this one huge family you could put together an autumn blaze as vivid as the eye can take. Many of the Japanese maples are dwarf and slow-growing, ideal for small gardens. Semi-shade suits them better than sun. *Acer palmatum* 'Osakazuki' is one of the most brilliant. The green dissected leaves turn brilliant scarlet and crimson in autumn. 'Senkaki' has similar shaped leaves, but they turn soft yellow. It also has excellent bark, the new growths a rich coral red. 'Bloodgood' is another *A. palmatum* variety with handsome, deeply dissected leaves, purple for most of the year, brilliant red in autumn. General habit, style of growth and leaf form should have as much to do with your choice as the autumn fling. That may only last for a week, if it happens at all, but you will have to look at the shrub for another 51 weeks. In terms of autumn performance, the maple family can be roughly divided into two teams : scarlet or clear, plain yellow. *Acer palmatum* var. heptalobum 'Lutescens' is a bushy-headed shrub with large five-lobed leaves that throw their lot in with the yellows. 'Chitoseyama' has a weeping habit of growth and plays for the reds.

The maples are not the only family that turn in a good autumn performance, but they are among the most accommodating. The ginkgo, or maidenhair tree, with notched, fan-like, leaves turns a glorious clear yellow in autumn, but this is a tree to treat with respect, not just because of its ancient lineage, but because it will eventually grow to 80ft/24m. It spreads endearingly with age. The liquidambar, or sweet gum, is not such an interesting tree, but colours more vividly in autumn in shades of orange and purple. If possible, you should see your plant before buying it. Some forms colour notably less well than others and without autumn colour, there would be little reason to grow this rather dense, overpowering tree.

Only in the biggest gardens will it be worth planting trees or shrubs that have nothing to say but their brief autumn statement. In most gardens, the October show must be made up of performers that can do a spring or summer act as good as their autumn one. The amelanchier planted for April effect will now dress itself overall with orange and red leaves. The pear 'Chanticleer', used for its blossom in May, has also got a good October turn up its sleeve when its foliage turns to red and maroon. Crab apples, also planted with spring flowers in mind, are now hung with masses of fruit, bright yellow in the variety 'Hornet', ox-blood red in the variety 'Liset'.

October's crop of fruit provides a second source of colour and delight this month, with crab apples and sorbuses at the top of the league. The sorbus family are cousins to the wild rowan or mountain ash. They will put up with drier conditions than crabs and seem to be more tolerant of air pollution. Birds snatch mountain ash berries almost before they have had time to ripen, but are not so quick to take the paler berries of the garden hybrids. *Sorbus vilmorinii* is an elegant member of the family, with feathery, ferny leaves, olive-green on top, paler underneath. In autumn these turn purple and red. The clusters of white blossom that have decorated the garden in June are now followed by dangling heads of small round berries, first red, then pink, then finally almost white. At dusk, the effect is remarkable, for the frame of the tree itself recedes into the shade while the berries shine out luminous against the darkening light. *Sorbus hupehensis* is another beauty, slightly taller than the other; about 15–20ft/4.5–6m. In autumn the leaves turn brilliant shades of red and orange while the fruits hang in pale ghostly clusters of pink and white. The berries have often set by late August, but they should persist long after the leaves have dropped. If this sounds too ethereal, you could plant *Sorbus* 'Joseph Rock' instead, an erect, compact tree like the rest of this tribe, with glossy green toothed leaves which turn russet red in autumn. It has bunches of cream flowers in May, followed by pale yellow berries which darken gradually as they age. By December they are almost the colour of amber.

Spindles are also fine trees for autumn fruit. One of them, *Euonymus europaeus*, is a native tree which you sometimes see in hedgerows, dashing in October with brilliant pink seed capsules which split open to show orange berries. 'Red Cascade' is an improved version of the wild tree. It has arching branches thickly covered with red seed capsules. The leaves also turn scarlet in a dramatic last fling before closing down for the winter. Spindles all make small trees, not more than about 10ft/3m high, which will grow in any sort of soil, even chalk. They do not make so much of a show in spring as the crabs or sorbus.

If you have no room for an extra tree specifically for October fruit, there are plenty of shrubs that berry exuberantly in autumn. Pyracantha may lack finesse, but that does not worry it at all. Nor should it worry us. At the time of year when it is at its most vivid (October onwards, if the birds leave it alone) there is little left in the garden with which it can clash. It responds well to formal training on house or garden walls. It is happy on a north or east aspect. Tie in as many whippy growths as you can this month. Cut out any that do not fit into the grand design in early summer, after the shrub has flowered. *P. coccinea* 'Lalandei' is a good variety with the usual hawthorn-like flowers and orange-red berries.

The cotoneasters are equally enthusiastic autumn berriers and can adapt to as many different growing conditions and positions as we can throw at them. They will hug the ground, arch high up into the air, spread themselves flat against a wall. Stick a pin anywhere in a list of them and you will find a good-tempered shrub with pleasant, often glossy leaves and masses of red berries (or yellow in the unusual *C. x rothschildianus*). Although its berries are tiny, the well-known *C. horizontalis* is one of the best of the family. It grows with splendid symmetry, side branches issuing from the main stem as stiff as a kipper's backbone. It is as happy on a horizontal as it is on a vertical plane and is useful where there is a difficult piece of steep ground to clothe. If you are looking for a taller variety, *C. bullatus* will grow up to 10ft/3m with glossy dark corrugated leaves, small pinky-white flowers in June and clusters of brilliant red oval-shaped berries from October onwards.

The last fling

There is another shrub which is strange and unusual enough to carry the October show on its own. This is *Callicarpa bodinieri* var. *giraldii* which has dense clusters of tiny round berries in the axils of the leaves. They are brilliant violet, and each is round and shiny like a bead. Its performance before autumn is undistinguished, but the autumn effect is stunning, particularly when the leaves have fallen and the berries are grouped in clusters up and down the bare upright branches. If you do not have room for a complete planting scheme for October, try and fit in this shrub somewhere on its own. If you do have a patch that you can devote to a special autumn display, make it the centrepiece of a group of plants that, unlike the callicarpa, will also make a contribution at other times of the year; the fine evergreen *Euphorbia characias wulfenii*, perhaps, and the neat crimson-flowered penstemon 'Garnet'. The penstemon's main display will start much earlier in the summer, of course, but there are usually stray spikes flowering into October if the weather is mild and the deep red is a splendid colour to see with the violet berries, the whole group backed by the glaucous foliage of the euphorbia. In the mind's eye, it is pleasant to think of the purple-apparelled callicarpa rising out of a frothy sea of grey – artemisia, perhaps, or soft lamb's ear. Unfortunately, by October the greys are looking their slimy, scruffy worst. It is the time of year when you realize, all too graphically, how much they would prefer to be back in their drier Mediterranean homes.

The callicarpa when fully grown will make a strongly upright shrub, no more than 6ft/1.8m high. The plain leaves have a brief moment of glory when they change to a violet-pink before dropping. The surprising berries are best seen against a fairly dark, plain background, perhaps an evergreen tree, or a fence covered in green ivy. If this is

1 *Callicarpa bodinieri*

DECIDUOUS SHRUB
HEIGHT AND SPREAD
6 x 6FT/1.8 x 1.8M
ZONE 6–8

The July flowers, clustered in the leaf axils round the stems of this shrub, make little impact, but their autumn metamorphosis is startling. Flowers turn to shining bead-like berries of an intense violet-purple. Nothing else has quite such startling fruit. The leaves turn shades of pink and purple before dropping. It thrives in any type of soil in a sunny position. It needs no regular pruning, but the bush can be reduced if necessary in February by cutting back some of the previous year's growth. Propagate by softwood cuttings taken with a heel in June or July.

2 *Euphorbia characias wulfenii* (**Spurge**)

EVERGREEN SUB-SHRUB
HEIGHT AND SPREAD
4 x 4FT/120 x 120CM
ZONE 7–9

One of the most splendid of all foliage plants, making a solid clump of many stems sprouting from the base. The stems have a biennial habit. For their first year, they make foliage. In the spring of their second year, they produce great domes of sulphurous yellow-green flowers above the leaves. Meanwhile new foliage shoots are being produced from the base. Cold spring winds may burn the foliage so try to give this euphorbia a position out of the worst draughts. Take care to untangle the roots of pot-grown plants when setting them out. Unless properly anchored, they are prone to toppling over and dying. Cut down flowered stems as they fade to leave room for new growth from the centre of the clump. Mulch with compost or well-rotted manure in spring.

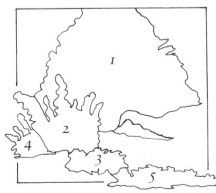

3 *Pulmonaria* (Lungwort)
DECIDUOUS PERENNIAL
HEIGHT AND SPREAD
12 X 18IN/30 X 45CM
ZONE 4–8

These are strong-growing plants, in full leaf between April and November. Flowers, in various shades of pink and blue, are borne on stems backed by small leaves during early spring. Plant from October to March in any decent garden soil. Leafy plants such as these need plenty of nitrogen, so mulch liberally in early spring to provide food and conserve moisture at the roots. Propagate by dividing plants in autumn or spring.

4 *Penstemon*
SEMI-EVERGREEN PERENNIAL
HEIGHT AND SPREAD
3 X 2FT/90 X 60CM
ZONE 8–10

Some cultivars of this desirable group are bigger than others. The popular 'Garnet' is middle of the range, hovering around 30in/75cm. All penstemons are beautiful, but unfortunately not reliably hardy. As a general rule of thumb, the larger the flower and leaf, the more tender the plant will be. 'Garnet' has narrow, fresh green foliage and is one of the tougher ones. It is a vigorous, bushy grower with a long flowering season, from June through until October. Damp is as

much an enemy as frost and it will do best in a well-drained spot in full sun. Do not cut down stems in autumn as this may encourage new shoots which will get slaughtered by frost. Stem cuttings taken in August and early September root easily and can be overwintered with protection. Low growths willingly layer themselves and these can be grown on.

5 *Crocus speciosus*
CORM
HEIGHT AND SPREAD
4 X 3IN/10 X 7.5CM
ZONE 5–9

In the wild this grows over a wide range from Eastern Europe across to Iran and the Caucasus. It has elegant flowers in a wide range of purples and mauves and also a pure white. The purplish ones have petals veined with darker colour and all have prominent, much divided stigma. Any of these colours will blend with the more startling purple berries of the callicarpa. Stick to one type or the effect will be dissipated. They usually appear for sale in autumn bulb catalogues and need to be planted as quickly as possible, setting them about 3in/7.5cm deep and 3–4 in/7.5–10cm apart. A pinch of bonemeal in the planting hole will provide all the necessary food. They are not fussy about soil, but like some sun in order to get a dry resting period during the summer. Grassy foliage follows the flowers in winter and spring.

difficult to arrange, bring in the euphorbia, *E. characias wulfenii*. You do not need an excuse to introduce this plant anyway. It is a superb perennial, evergreen, architectural and the biggest member of a family that could play a part in several of the planting schemes suggested for the first half of the year. In spring, it explodes with massive flower heads, hundreds of sulphur-yellow bracts clustered round the end of the flowering stem. By October you will have cleared the remains of the flower stems away and will be left with a fine mound of foliage, up to 4ft/1.2m high and as much across. The leaves, the blue side of green, are arranged in whorls around the stems, which are thick and succulent, sometimes tinged with red. Although it is a native of Europe, the plant has a somewhat tropical air, but its rounded shape and the easy way it holds itself make it an undaunting neighbour. It makes a good background for the callicarpa, whose berries intensify the blueness of the spurge's leaves. The new growth at the extremities is particularly glaucous and holds raindrops entire and globular in separate drops.

The penstemon's virtues have already been described in a planting scheme for August, where the large blue cultivar 'Alice Hindley' was used. Here, the smaller, more compact old variety 'Garnet' is what is called for, now at the end of its generous flowering, but still able to contribute a dash of deep red to the scheme. 'Garnet' has thin, neat leaves and a tidy habit. Although no penstemon can be relied on in the matter of winter hardiness, size of leaf and flower give a rough indication of their chances. 'Garnet' is relatively small in both respects. It grows so eagerly that, even if top growth is cut back by frosts, it will quickly make up lost ground. *P. barbatus* would also fit well into this scheme, though the red flowers are more scarlet than wine. Spring is sometimes more treacherous than winter, especially where the penstemon is exposed to drying winds. Try to make sure that it is not. Hedge your bets by taking cuttings in late summer and overwintering them with some protection. There is another good reason for bringing on a constant succession of new plants. Youngsters have a longer flowering season than established clumps, which concentrate most of their efforts into the summer display. For this October group, you need plants that are willing to do more than that.

If there is room for more in this autumn group, use clumps of a good variegated pulmonaria, perhaps divisions of the one you may have used with hellebores and magnolia in March, perhaps an entirely different kind. There are many from which to choose and since the leaf markings vary so dramatically, even on plants that are supposed to be the same variety, it is worth choosing carefully. In spring, the pulmonaria was used for its sprays of pinky-blue flowers, but it is also a handsome and long-lasting foliage plant. Pulmonarias are tolerant, undemanding creatures although they may whinge if they are left to bake in full sun on dry soil through the summer. They do best in cool, rich soil with some shade.

The final addition to this group is a scattering of the fragile-looking autumn crocus, *C. speciosus*. This has elegant, long-petalled flowers of purple-blue, veined with a network of darker blue. The central stigmas are brilliant orange. Flowers usually begin appearing before the end of September. Grassy leaves follow on during winter and spring. It is not a difficult plant to please, but you need at least two dozen of them to make any impact. 'Oxonian' is a good dark form, 'Aitchisonii' is large, and a pale lavender colour.

Fruits and seeds

Growing a rose for its hips may seem as contrary as growing a runner bean for its flowers, but at this time of the year, you notice what a stunning effect one good fruiting rose can have in the garden. The blue-leaved rose *R. glauca* (syn. *R. rubrifolia*) has self-effacing single pink flowers in summer, but clusters of eye catching shiny red hips in autumn. The best known hippy rose is *R. moyesii* which has long flagon-shaped fruit that hang like Christmas tree decorations from the branches. The five sepals of the dead flowers make a crown at the end of each hip. 'Geranium' is a selection which has orange-red flowers rather than its parent's deep crimson flowers and the hips are a paler colour. 'Highdownensis' is another *R. moyesii* hybrid with excellent hips and light crimson flowers. Both these hybrids are less vigorous than their parent, making upright, arching shrubs, ultimately 8ft/2.4m high and 5ft/1.5m wide. They can be contained by regularly cutting out some of the oldest branches at the base in spring. In general, the best rose-hips come from species roses rather than hybrids, but there are exceptions. The Gallica hybrid 'Scharlachglut' has splendid large urn-shaped fruit, each with a persistent spidery calyx. The climbing Hybrid Tea 'Mme Gregoire Staechelin', with large, pale pink flowers, has good orange-red hips if it is not dead-headed. Either *R. glauca* or *R. moyesii* can be used as the centrepiece of an October grouping of rose, honesty, salvia – one of the brilliant blue late-flowering species such as *S. cacaliifolia* – and *Iris foetidissima*, whose yawning seed-pods are now displaying their own crop of brilliant autumn berries. Space may dictate which rose you choose. *R. glauca* is slightly more compact in growth and tops out at 6ft/1.8m. Both are tolerant of some shade, though will flower and therefore fruit better in full sun. Both are tolerant of poor soils and neither will give more than one flush of flowers between mid-June and mid-July. *R. glauca* has the better foliage, but less showy hips.

The honesty, which in May will have had heads of magenta-purple flowers, has

1 *Rosa moyesii* 'Geranium'

DECIDUOUS SHRUB

HEIGHT AND SPREAD

8 x 5 FT/2.4 x 1.5 M

ZONE 6–9

The best of the various *R. moyesii* selections, with single orange-red flowers and a central boss of creamy anthers. In October it is hung with shiny flagon-shaped hips, deep red and larger than those of ordinary *R. moyesii*. It is tolerant of shade and poor soil, but obviously will do better with neither. If you plant in poor soil, give the rose a good start in a decent-sized hole with plenty of well-rotted muck mixed in with the soil. Mulch well each spring. No regular pruning is necessary, but the shrub can be reduced by cutting out some of the older wood each spring.

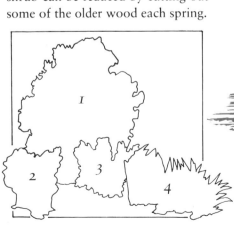

2 Lunaria annua (Honesty)

BIENNIAL
HEIGHT AND SPREAD
30 X 12 IN/75 X 30 CM
ZONE 5–9

This is a fast-growing plant with coarse-toothed heart-shaped leaves. The flowers are four-petalled and range from a rich magenta to a pure white, which comes true from seed. In October there are flat silver seedheads. Sow seed outside in a nursery bed in May or June. Thin out the seedlings or transplant them at 6in/15cm intervals and grow them on for planting out in September.

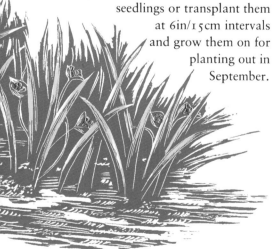

3 Salvia cacaliifolia

SEMI-EVERGREEN PERENNIAL
HEIGHT AND SPREAD
3 X 3 FT/90 X 90 CM
ZONE 5–10

All the salvias are sun-lovers, and this must be kept in mind when you are planting. This unusual species is an elegant though leafy thing, with racemes of brilliant blue-lipped flowers from late summer until the first frosts. Like many of the new salvias being introduced from Mexico and other hotspots, it is not fully hardy in this country. Top growth may get cut down, in ordinary perennial fashion, but a tough winter may finish it off

altogether. You forgive its leafiness, because the foliage is smart, stiff, bright green, and the leaves broadly triangular. It needs sun and will droop gracefully, layering its stems on top of one another to make a bright skirt of green. Propagate it from cuttings in late September and October and overwinter these under cover as an insurance against loss. You will have no trouble using them.

4 Iris foetidissima (Stinking iris, gladdon)

EVERGREEN PERENNIAL
HEIGHT AND SPREAD
2 X 2 FT/60 X 60 CM
ZONE 6–9

Clumps of sword-shaped leaves grow from a fleshy underground rhizome and being bright and evergreen, provide useful winter window dressing. The flowers are insignificant, mauve in the standard species, lemon yellow in the variety 'Citrina'. The seed pods on the branched stem split in October to reveal brilliant orange seeds, so heavy that the stem is often bowed down by their weight. Thrives in a wide variety of conditions, including bog and dry shade. Its common name comes from the smell of its leaves when crushed. Plant in autumn, setting the rhizomes just beneath the surface of the soil. Like all irises, it will take some time to settle down before it flowers. Increase by lifting and dividing rhizomes in October. They need no special feeding. Cut down the seed-heads when the berries have all gone.

now dried and faded to a bleached white skeleton, all foliage gone and the flowers turned to the familiar flat silver discs that children use as make-believe money. The seed is flattened against a translucent central membrane and protected by two outer discs, not quite so ethereal, but palest buff. They stand well all through the early part of winter. Once you have introduced honesty into your garden, you usually have it for ever. Its proper name is *Lunaria annua*, which is confusing as it is actually a biennial. The first year it makes a low plant, all leaf and lushness. In its second year, it shoots up to flower and then into seed. There is a very pretty variegated version, but the flowers are a muddy mauve and the plant does not persist naturally in the way that the plain-leaved type does. The plain *L. annua* has flowers in a variety of colours from deep purple to white.

Salvia cacaliifolia is as rare as the honesty is common. It has excellent thick leathery leaves with a slight sheen, broadly triangular in shape. The flowers, which start very late in the season, are the same intense blue as *Salvia patens*, but they are smaller and borne in terminal spikes. Each one looks flattened, as though it had been pinched together between finger and thumb. It is two-lipped, like the *S. patens* flower, but not so prominently beaky. It has an elegant habit of growth, with side branches drooping slightly from the main stem and the leaves displaying themselves stiffly and prominently the whole of the length. It is in no way a showy plant, but certainly an aristocratic one. Once you have had it, you will be sorry to be without it. If you want the blue working further back in the group, choose one of the tall salvias such as *S. guaranitica*. It is a rangy grower, up to five feet and comes from Brazil. It has brilliantly blue flowers that yawn like the pictures of hippopotamuses you see on television wildlife programmes. It is no more reliably hardy than any of the other salvias. Less intense blue, more sky-coloured is *Salvia uliginosa*. Its name suggests it likes bogs, but it does not seem too distressed by dry summer weather. Whereas the upper and lower jaws of *S. guaranitica*'s flowers are equally matched, *S. uliginosa* has a splayed bottom lip and a mere remnant of a top lip, whitish rather than blue. Each individual flower is tiny, but they mass together at the end of graceful, five foot stems.

The iris, with its bright green sword-shaped leaves, will provide a strong foliage contrast with the honesty and salvia, but neither its foliage nor its flowers are as good as its autumn display of berries. Its sausage-shaped seed pods burst into three segments in early autumn to reveal fatly packed rows of shiny berries, the brilliant colour of sealing wax. Once established, it will seed itself about harmlessly and is useful in dry shade. The flowers, minimal muddy purple, come out in June, but you may never notice them, what with everything else that is going on in the garden at that time. A variety called

'Citrina' has ochre-yellow flowers, elegantly etched in brown and these, though still small, have more to recommend them.

The whole of this group could be set in front of a parthenocissus for a wild autumn conflagration, but you must choose these creepers with care. The more rampant ones, *P. quinquefolia*, the true Virginia creeper, or *P. tricuspidata* (Boston ivy) are only suitable for very large gardens. They clothe areas very quickly, which may be at the outset an advantage. This is quickly offset by the disadvantage of fighting them every year thereafter, as they throttle other plants, bring down fences and block gutters. Choose one of the less bold colonizers such as *P. henryana* with dark, velvety green leaves, the midrib and veins etched with white. It colours, but not quite as vividly as the rampant varieties. The most spectacular of the autumn-colouring vines, *Vitis coignetiae*, is also greedy for space, but slightly easier to control as it does not stick to things with the chewing-gum sucker pads that Virginia creeper has, but hoists itself about with tendrils that curl round whatever they touch.

Now and again, October comes up trumps with a whole series of rich, warm, still days that provide you with some of the best gardening conditions of the whole year. There is an element of lottery about such days. Each one, you feel, might be the last. Nothing can be taken for granted. This might be the last day you see the salvias in bloom. This might be the last chance to clap your nose to one of the long scented trumpets of the white tobacco flower *Nicotiana sylvestris*, or cut bunches of outrageous dahlias for the house. Make the most of them.

WINTER

SYBARITES MAY FEEL THAT THE WINTER GARDEN IS A PLACE ONLY FOR masochists, and will be happy to concentrate their efforts on constructing a palace of pleasure from April to September. There are delights in a winter garden, however, though they are more muted than summer's effects. For this period, the principle of grouping plants together for seasonal effect is abandoned. Special winter effects can be scattered round the garden as beacons, talismans to reassure you that there is life out there under the swirls of November fog, the gloom of December afternoons, the frosts of January and the bleak, wet, windy days of February. Winter's performers are a more subdued cast than summer's, with white and pink and mauve dominating the colour scale, but an unexpected fragility, or glorious scent, as with daphne, makes them particularly valuable at this season. Daphnes, hellebores, snowdrops, viburnums, with the yellow of aconites, jasmine and mahonia, and some of the early crocus, are the chief players. In large gardens, the possibilities increase. There will be room for stands of contrasting dogwoods, scarlet stems interspersed with khaki-yellow ones. There will be space to experiment with catkins, for sometimes, when you round a corner in a country lane and come upon a hazel in the hedge, dripping with soft golden catkins, you wonder why on earth such a fuss should ever be made about Chinese chimonanthus or hamamelis when we have such elegant natives to hand.

Winter is often a time of reckoning, particularly with regard to a garden's balance and design. When summer trimmings are stripped away, the winter garden reveals its bones, or lack of them. This is when you realize, all too graphically, why it is that gardening writers are endlessly wagging their fingers about the importance of evergreens in the garden. In summer, whirling in a perpetual dance with mock orange, roses, clematis and lilies, you are inclined to mutter rebelliously 'A fig for your evergreens'. Now in winter, deserted by the dizzy flower throng, the garden reduced to an amorphous tangle of buff and brown, your defiance may seem self-defeating. Evergreen does not mean any evergreen in any quantity and it rarely means x *Cupressocyparis leylandii*. There are many reasons not to plant this Leyland cypress. It is characterless. It is depressing. Like a cuckoo in the nest, it almost always outgrows its home, engaging its keepers in an exhausting battle with shears, loppers and saw to keep its greedy branches from taking all light and all space to itself. Few trees look as uncomfortable in our landscape as the Leyland cypress. Cemeteries and electricity sub-stations may provide satisfactory settings for its blank, soulless bulk, but a garden – no.

Leylands do not change with the seasons, they have no blossom and no fruit to speak of. This charge could be levelled at a large number of evergreens, but what singles out the Leyland is that it has neither shape nor shine to its leaves and no overall architecture at all. In harsh winds, particularly those with a tinge of sea salt in them, they wither and brown in a most unsightly way. What they *can* do is grow, sometimes up to 2ft/60cm a year. If you are figuring out a way to fit in your winter evergreens and at the same time fighting to establish some privacy in a pocket handkerchief of a plot, surrounded by nosy neighbours, this may seem a great advantage. And so it may be, for the first three years or so. After that, it is a curse. For each extra couple of feet that the thing reaches into the sky, there is a corresponding shadow on the ground. Before long, the whole handkerchief may be cast in gloom, confined in a suffocating, dark green prison. There is another disadvantage. Since the spread of a mature Leyland is about 15ft/4.5m, you will also lose a great deal of your garden and the overwhelming bulk will completely swamp any planting schemes that you may be planning for summer.

In a small town garden, neat topiary shapes of box will be sufficient to carry through the evergreen theme, supported perhaps by some flamboyant camellias and a scattering of good foliage plants. Box balls balanced in tubs either side of steps, or pyramids by a doorway, or a helter-skelter spiral sitting in a large pot at the end of the view from the main window can do wonders for a winter scene. The advantage of having evergreens in tubs is that each season they can be tried in different positions, altering the emphasis of the garden and drawing the eye to different juxtapositions. The simplest method (though expensive) is to buy specimens already trained. Then your only task will be to clip them over neatly each year in August or September. Though box and yew are the species traditionally chosen for topiary, there are other evergreens that respond equally well to clipping. Bay and Portugal laurel both make excellent lollipops, bay with the added advantage of furnishing the kitchen with bouquets garnis. Ilex, the evergreen oak, is suitable for work on a grander scale. It makes, in any form, a handsome tree, with dark olive-green leaves backed with silver, but it is breathtaking when clipped, as it is in the east garden at Hatfield House, into a double avenue of tall, clean-stemmed trunks, each topped with a sphere of evergreen leaves, the most stylish topiary in England.

Certain trees suggest certain types of training. Box and yew, because they are both small-leaved, can be made into the most complicated shapes. Holly, because it has a natural habit of throwing out branches in tiers at regular intervals up the stem, is often clipped into cake-stand shapes, with a round top-knot or finial to complete the structure. Golden variegated hollies are just as suitable for this kind of treatment as plain green ones. Hollies in any form, clipped or free growing, make perhaps the handsomest of winter trees, even when stripped of their berries as they usually are before Christmas. Think carefully, however, before buying the golden variegated forms for a small garden. You may find, particularly if you have a penchant for pink and mauve flowers in summer, that it gets in the way then, though undoubtedly more showy than its green cousins in winter. Only the female kinds bear berries and there must, somewhere in the vicinity, even if not in your garden, be a male variety to do the pollinating. The names, as you will discover, are no use in sorting one from another. 'Silver Queen' is a transvestite. So is 'Golden King', though the gender-bending is reversed. 'J. C. van Tol' is one of the few varieties that does not need cross-fertilizing in order to set a good crop of berries. It has handsome plain green leaves and stems that are dark purple when young. It grows about 20ft/6m high and is one of the best of the hollies to use as a free-standing tree.

Evergreenness does not have to come only from trees. Ivy is an invaluable winter ally for it is a dog with many tricks. It can climb 100ft/30m or more without getting dizzy. It can hang upside down from urns and tubs without the sap rushing to its head. It can turn breeze-block walls and chain-link fences into things of beauty, which is perhaps the cleverest trick of all. It is handsome and as a garden plant, hugely under-used. This may be because, like holly and hazel, fellow natives, we take it too much for granted. Ivy can be used, almost as a muralist might use it, to make arches or other shapes on a plain whitewashed wall, giving architectural detail to what otherwise might be a too plain basement yard. Maintenance is not taxing. Trained ivy will need a twice-yearly clip in late February and July to keep clean outlines. If there is little bare soil round the roots, as is often the case when ivies are used on paved courtyard walls, give plants a monthly feed of liquid fertilizer between April and September and an occasional hosing down with a fine spray of water if the leaves begin to look dusty in summer. There are several hundred varieties available, some with severely botanical names such as 'Minor Marmorata' and 'Sagittifolia Variegata' and others that sound like fancy ice-creams – 'Lemon Swirl' and 'Green Ripple'.

Some ivies are better at trailing than climbing. Some are particularly good for ground cover. If you are looking at a blank wall that you want to cover with ivy for winter interest, buy enough plants to set them 2ft/60cm apart. It is tempting to pin growths of new plants to the wall and stand over them shouting 'Cling, cling !', but they will not listen. Instead, plant them a little way out from the wall and lay the trails along the ground, anchoring them with U-bends of wire or small stones. If the ground beneath them is reasonably friable, the trails will root at the leaf joints. The new growth that starts from these points will cling as tight as a latex jumpsuit. For climbing, try the variegated Persian ivy *Hedera colchica* 'Dentata Variegata', dark-leaved *H. helix* 'Atropurpurea', the beautifully formed 'Fleur-de-Lis' or the bird's foot ivy, *H. helix* 'Pedata'. Ivy will have no ill effect on mortar that is in good condition, but it will start nibbling into the gaps around old loose mortar and loosen it even more. It will poke fingers between the boards of a wooden slatted fence which eventually will be strong enough to prise the boards apart.

Where ivies are to be used as ground cover, and this is one of their most useful winter roles, swirling perhaps around clumps of snowdrops under a tree, or filling a gap between border and boundary where little else shows an inclination to flourish, the same rule applies as with any other ground-cover plant. Begin with clean ground. Ivies are slow starters and will be entirely discouraged if they have to argue the toss with bindweed, couch and horsetail. If you are planting on a steep bank, it may help to use pots with the bottoms knocked out. Sink the pots into the bank, fill them with a good, rich compost such as John Innes No. 3 and plant the ivies inside the pots, which will prevent the soil getting washed from around them. You can also plant through black polythene sheet, but the disadvantage of this is that stems will not be able to root as they go and growth will be less vigorous. Most ivies are pot-grown and so can be planted at any time of the year. For ground cover, choose the silver-grey 'Glacier', 'Ivalace' which has prettily indented leaves, or the German variety 'Konigers Auslese' which has small narrow leaves, but a lot of them.

Use ivies under a big tree set in a lawn, where grass may be scrappy and starved. Use it on the steep, difficult slope that semi-basement windows often look on to. Use it between shrubs in a half-shaded planting. Use it as fake topiary to cover an arbour. Ivy responds well to clipping and has the advantage of being much faster-growing than yew or box. It will be most effective when seen in contrast with brick, or stone, or bark, so keep growth in check. Ivy lapping up to the bottom of a clean stone wall will have more impact than greenery that covers both ground and wall. The trunk of a yew or beech is as architectural as a cathedral pillar rising cleanly out of a bed of ivy. The contrast in texture will be lost if ivy masks the bark. On the other hand, a few tendrils of ivy curling round the base of a statue, pot or urn makes it an instant antique and anchors it convincingly to its site. Tinkering with ivy in this way is a pleasant winter task. Remember however that you can only take off, not put on, and use secateurs cautiously.

The wild arum or cuckoo pint has a garden relative, *Arum italicum pictum*, which is a superb winter foliage plant. The leaves have the distinctive crinkled arrow-shape of the wild plant, but each leaf is heavily marbled in silver along the veins and midrib. Only a thin border round the edge of each leaf is plain green. The furled spikes of the first leaves push through in November and fresh growth continues through the winter. The leaves die back by early June, leaving an evil-looking spathe which by September is clustered with brilliant red berries. It likes a rich, moist soil in sun or light shade and is excellent in January and February in between clumps of snowdrops. It is about 12in/ 30cm high and clumps gradually thicken up to 12in/30cm or more wide.

Spotty laurel (*Aucuba japonica*) is undeservedly ignored as a winter foliage shrub. Victorians overdosed on aucuba and consequently for years afterwards this stalwart of winter gardens was rather despised. It is a handsome glossy thing however and very tolerant of the dust and pollution that hang over some inner city gardens. There are still about 17 different varieties available. 'Crotonifolia', with large leaves boldly blotched with gold, is one of the best. It is male and if you want the red berries that brighten the shrub's winter uniform, plant a female such as 'Gold Dust', also variegated with gold. The adapt well to life in tubs. If you need to restrict growth, cut old shoots hard back in spring. Plant in spring or autumn in any reasonable soil in sun or shade. Plants in tubs will need regular liquid feeds from May to September.

The superb spurge, *Euphorbia characias wulfenii* has a double-barrelled name because nobody seems to be quite sure whether it is one or the other. Some say that *E. characias* has a dark eye to the flower while *E. c. wulfenii* does not. Botanists may fuss, but gardeners will be happy with either. Characteristically the plant makes an important mound of evergreen foliage, up to 4ft/120cm high and wide, with a succulent, slightly foreign quality about it. The blue-grey leaves, the size and shape of a little finger, are arranged in whorls around thick fleshy stems. After the first frosts the tips of the stems that are going to flower bend over and have the inquisitive, slightly imperious quality of a band of chickens. By the end of January, the first hints of sulphurous yellow will already be apparent in the flowers. They do not come into full glory until later in the spring, when the flower heads begin to grow and unfurl into upright dense columns. At its zenith, it is overwhelming. Few other plants have the personality to stand up to it. It is excellent used at the corner of a bed, or at the junction of terrace and step. If you use it near a path, bear in mind its full adult size when you are planting. Seedlings look rather puny, but once they start eating their porridge, grow at a satisfying rate. It is far too fine a plant to be chipping away at in order to keep a free passage. The only cutting you need to do is to remove the old flower stems in early summer before they get in the way of the new growth pushing up from the centre of the clump.

Essential evergreens

The foliage of several cyclamen, including *C. hederifolium*, continues to look magnificent through the winter, seemingly untroubled by frost and low enough to be untouched by gales. If you have not already pressed the cyclamen into service in one of the schemes suggested for September, you can use it as one of the components in a winter group that will continue to hold interest for the rest of the year. Use as a centrepiece one of the tall-growing mahonias, either *M. x media* 'Charity' which has rich yellow flowers in upright spikes borne between November and February, or the slightly better form *M. x* 'Lionel Fortescue', a different child of the same parents that produced 'Charity'. The chief delight of these shrubs, whichever variety you choose, is not the flowers, nor even their heady smell – though that is heartwarming enough on a dire November day to make you bless the shrub's existence. The best thing about these tall mahonias is their shape, both the overall form and the sharp, spiky outline of the pinnate leaves, carried in ruffs around the gaunt stems. Each leaf is about 12in/30cm long, made up of a strong central midrib with up to nine pairs of holly-like leaflets arranged along it, with a single leaflet giving a terminal flourish. It is not a comfortable shrub. It is gaunt, stark and uncompromising. It is an Enoch Powell among shrubs. Left to itself, it adopts a strongly vertical habit of growth, so that before long, flowers burst open way above your head and you are left with nothing to look at but the striated bark. You can curb this tendency by firmly pruning each stem after flowering to bring it back down to eye level. Mahonias like shade, as do the rest of this small winter-flowering group.

Around the mahonia, plant clumps of hellebores, perhaps forms of *H. orientalis*, whose flowers will begin to open by the middle of January and still will look good by the middle of April. The hellebores are weird flowers – and very cultish ones. Once, you had to put your child's name down at birth if you wanted him to get into Eton or Harrow. You have to do much the same thing to get hold of a new cultivar of the Lenten hellebore. They are slow to raise from seed and plants resent the disturbance caused by dividing. Fortunately, *any* kind of *H. orientalis* is worth having, whether the pale kinds, the insides

1 *Mahonia x media* 'Lionel Fortescue'

EVERGREEN SHRUB
HEIGHT AND SPREAD
8 X 9 FT/2.5 X 2.8 M
ZONE 8–9

Some find mahonias an acquired taste, for they are spiky, odd shrubs, but wonderfully handsome in winter, with their holly-like leaflets arranged along stiff midribs. The habit of growth is naturally very upright. Without judicious pruning after

flowering, you may find that all the action is above your head. The flowers are carried in upright racemes, yellow and heavily scented. Shade or at least half shade is the best place for it. Mulch heavily in spring. Propagate by tip cuttings in July.

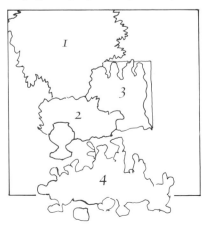

2 Helleborus orientalis

EVERGREEN PERENNIAL
HEIGHT AND SPREAD
24 X 24 IN/60 X 60 CM
ZONE 4–8

These are the most gorgeous flowers of winter, minutely varied in colour and patterning, but all mysterious, ideal ingredients for a witch's brew. The leaves are hand-shaped, stiff and glossy and continue to please long after the flowers have finished. In most districts, the old leaves of this handsome perennial stand in reasonable condition until the flower stems push through in February and March. Then the spent foliage can be cut away before it is replaced with the new young leaves which follow the flowers. The saucer-shaped heads look down towards the ground. Crimson, purple, pink and white forms are available, together with some extremely expensive named varieties. Many have complicated markings inside the petals. Plant in October in part shade in deep, well-drained, moist soil and then leave them alone.

3 Hedera helix 'Adam'

EVERGREEN CLIMBER
HEIGHT AND SPREAD
12 X 12 FT/3.5 X 3.5 M
ZONE 6–7

Ivies are endlessly versatile plants, happy to go up or down or to scrabble around at ground level. They have the useful ability to flourish in deep shade, where little else is willing to show its nose. Even an ivy appreciates good food from time to time and a generous annual mulch will have an explosive effect on the plant's growth rate. Starved, they can be very slow to make ground. Summer watering also helps. In winter the pale variegated types such as 'Glacier' and

'Adam' shine out against plain evergreens. 'Adam' is variegated in white and cream. After frost, the foliage is sometimes tinged with pink. It is strongly resistant to reverting to plain green and is very hardy. Plant in well-fed soil between September and March. Propagate by tip cuttings in July or take six-inch cuttings of ripe wood in October or November.

4 Cyclamen coum

CORM
HEIGHT AND SPREAD
3 X 10 IN/8 X 25 CM
ZONE 6–9

Cyclamen only flourish in soil that is high in organic matter. Do not try to grow them in hot, starved soil. Leaf-mould is ideal for digging into the earth before planting. Bonemeal, added at planting time, also gives them a boost. The leathery rounded leaves are dark green, an excellent foil for the stubby pink flowers that appear from December to March. There are also attractive variegated forms, with leaves silvered in the manner of their autumn-flowering cousins, *C. hederifolium*. The shape of the leaf is unchanged. The plants are very small and are best used towards the front of any planting scheme, where you can appreciate the elegant flowers. They are sometimes more difficult to establish than *C. hederifolium*, but well worth the effort. Plant no deeper than an inch. Seed can be collected and sown in September in pans to overwinter.

of the flowers freckled in green, or the deep purple, almost black kinds, sinister enough to make the major ingredients in a witch's brew. They are particularly useful because although not strictly evergreen, they never leave a bare patch. The flower buds push through the stems of the old leaves in December and this is the time to cut the old leaves away. As the flowers begin to fade, new leaves begin to grow up round them and these last, glossily splendid, until the cycle begins all over again the following winter. The flowers droop on their stems in a bell-like way. To admire the full complexity of the markings on the inside of the petals, you will have to go down on your knees, entirely appropriate in front of this plant. There are five broad petals and a central boss of creamy stamens. The texture of the petals is thick and waxen and the stippling of colour as complicated as a bird's feathering. Although subdued, they are supremely elegant flowers and the foliage that lasts for the whole of the year is handsome also – hand-shaped leaves of glossy green, each held at the end of a stout stem rising from the ground.

Behind the mahonia, plant a clump of ivy – not one of the strident sulphur or gold variegated ones, but something cool like the neat grey and cream variety 'Adam', which has small pale olive-coloured leaves. 'Glacier' has rather larger leaves with the same cool colouring. If there is a wall or fence conveniently to hand, the ivy can be planted to climb up this. Otherwise it will ramble around gently on the ground. In front of the hellebores add a dozen or so corms of the winter-flowering cyclamen, *C. coum*. In the wild, this is an extremely variable species, found in Bulgaria, along the shores of the Black Sea, in Northern Iran, Syria and Lebanon. The garden forms we most commonly see have rounded leaves, dark shiny green, and flowers of magenta, pale pink and white. All have a deep magenta blotch at the base of the petals. The flowers are stubbier than those of *C. hederifolium*, and, of course, borne at the same time as the leaves, in January and February, whereas *C. hederifolium* sends its flowers as an advance party before it produces any foliage. There are several forms with blotched or almost entirely silver leaves. In the wild, the silvered forms are found more often in the east, Syria and Lebanon, than they are in western habitats. Both seem equally hardy and the colours of the flowers blend beautifully with the mottled pinks and purples of the hellebore flowers nodding over them. In the wild, this cyclamen chooses shaded or semi-shaded places to grow in pine and oak forests, or lodges itself into crevices and ravines of rock. Good drainage is obviously important in the garden. If you have chosen the plain dark-leaved form of *C. coum*, contrast it with clumps of *C. hederifolium*, with handsome marbled leaves in green and silver. The flowers will have finished back in the autumn, but the leaves are at their best now, compact mounds of foliage rising from the underground corms that may be as big as dinner plates. Small self-sown seedlings of this cyclamen will be showing up now, too – spindly single leaves held on a thread-like stem and growing from a corm no bigger than a peppercorn, but surprisingly tough. These five elements – mahonia, ivy, hellebores and the two sorts of cyclamen – will make a long-lasting winter group with enough innate grace to see it through summer too.

Extolling the virtues of bark (deep, fissured texture, vibrant claret overtones) brings one dangerously close to the realms of *Private Eye*'s Pseud's Corner, but it is nevertheless a delight, albeit a quiet one, of the winter garden. The Edwardian gardener E. A. Bowles was a bark fanatic and used to go out with a bucket and brush to scrub the trunks of his yew trees in order to intensify the colour. Looked at in detail, yew bark is indeed extraordinary, bloody red and cinnamon brown with fifty unnameable shades in between. Winter rain intensifies the colours. Deciduous trees, bared in winter, show off their bark even better than evergreens. Two families are paramount in the winter bark stakes : maples and birches, and if you pick the right varieties, both are light-boned enough to tuck into gardens without dominating them. There is a whole group of maples which are lumped together under the epithet 'snake-bark'. It is a fair description of the effect – trunks variously striped in green and white. *Acer davidii* is typical. It has grey-green bark with white striations, smooth and pleasing. It grows to about 20ft/6m. *A. grosseri* is similar. So is *A. pensylvanicum* and none of them will overpower even the smallest garden. The maples have another winter trick, particularly noticeable in the species *A. griseum*. This has bark that curls away from the trunk in papery flakes to reveal new bark underneath, the old and the young bark darker and lighter shades of cinnamon. The shrubby coral bark maple *A. palmatum* 'Senkaki' has branches of a conspicuous coral red. Just one of these, underplanted perhaps with aconites which will bring out the warm tones of the bark, will do wonders for a winter garden.

Birches have wide-spreading surface roots and are greedier trees to accommodate in a small garden than the maples. They have lighter foliage though and riveting white stems. The whitest of all is the Himalayan variety *Betula utilis jacquemontii* which, when it is mature, will reach 30ft/9m. It is named after a young French naturalist, Victor Jacquemont, who botanized in the early years of the nineteenth century. In the wild, birches grow on rather poor acid heathland and in the garden seem to associate most naturally with other acid-loving plants, heathers, rhododendrons, camellias. For a dazzling display to warm the heart of any manufacturer of detergent, underplant your birch with patches of snowdrops.

The gardener in winter must not lose heart in the general miasma of rotting lambs' ears and blighted forget-me-nots. The thing to do is to develop tunnel vision, so that you see the viburnum blossoming on its bare stems and miss the piptanthus, whose evergreen leaves may well be blackened by frost or cutting winds. But what did you expect ? The tender piptanthus, a child of balmier climates, was not told by its mother what to do about frosts and cold winds. You must hone the ability to dwell on the pleasant prospect of *Crocus chrysanthus* in full bloom one day, even if the next day it is dashed to pieces by a hailstorm. From time to time there will be hiccups : devilish frosts, malevolent winds that may in one night smash your dreams, fell an important tree, kill outright a fine ceanothus that you have spent a dozen years training over the front of your house. But there have been other winds and other frosts – and other gardeners, centuries ago, who undaunted by loss went on to plant the cedars and the yews and the stands of beech that seem as though they have been there for ever. Disaster strengthens resolve and once you have recovered from the first blow, you know you can recover from the next. The true disaster is not to have lost the tulip tree or the rose or your prize peonies, crushed under your neighbour's blown-over fence ; it is to fail to replant them.

PLANT DIARY

	FEBRUARY	MARCH	APRIL	MAY	JUNE
Abelia	Mulch	Plant	Plant		
Acanthus		Plant	Feed		
Agapanthus			Plant	Feed	
Alchemilla		Transplant	Transplant		
Allium				Feed	
Amelanchier		Mulch			
Anaphalis		Divide	Plant	Trim	
Anemone blanda					
Anemone japonica		Divide	Feed		
Anemone nemorosa					
Aquilegia		Plant			
Argyranthemum				Plant	
Artemisia			Plant		
Aster		Divide	Feed		
Astrantia		Divide	Feed		
Baptisia			Feed		
Bellis		Divide			Sow
Brunnera		Plant	Feed		
Calendula			Sow		
Callicarpa	Prune	Plant	Mulch		
Camellia		Plant	Mulch		
Campanula		Mulch	Divide		
Caryopteris		Prune	Mulch		
Ceratostigma		*Prune	Plant		
Chaenomeles		Mulch		Prune	
Cheiranthus					Sow

*An asterisk indicates that this is optional, but not essential.

JULY	AUGUST	SEPTEMBER	OCTOBER	NOVEMBER	
Cuttings			*Prune		**Abelia**
			Divide	Cut down	**Acanthus**
			Cut down	Protect	**Agapanthus**
			Plant	Cut down	**Alchemilla**
			Feed	Divide	**Allium**
				Plant	**Amelanchier**
			Cut down		**Anaphalis**
	Divide	Plant	Plant	Feed	**Anemone blanda**
			Plant	Cut down	**Anemone japonica**
				Feed	**Anemone nemorosa**
Feed	Sow		Plant	Plant	**Aquilegia**
	Cuttings				**Argyranthemum**
	Cuttings		Cut down		**Artemisia**
Stake			Plant	Cut down	**Aster**
			Plant	Cut down	**Astrantia**
			Plant	Cut down	**Baptisia**
		Plant			**Bellis**
	Divide			Cut down	**Brunnera**
					Calendula
Cuttings			Plant		**Callicarpa**
Cuttings					**Camellia**
			Plant	Cut down	**Campanula**
	Cuttings		Plant		**Caryopteris**
Cuttings			Mulch		**Ceratostigma**
Cuttings			Plant		**Chaenomeles**
			Plant		**Cheiranthus**

	FEBRUARY	MARCH	APRIL	MAY	JUNE
Clematis alpina		Mulch	Mulch	*Prune	
Clematis macropetala		Plant	Mulch		
Clematis 'Perle d'Azur'	Prune	Mulch			
Clematis viticella		Prune	Plant	Mulch	
Convallaria					
Corylopsis		Mulch	Mulch		
Cotinus	Layer	Prune	Mulch		
Crataegus	Sow				
Crocus					
Crocus speciosus					
Cyclamen coum					
Cyclamen hederifolium					Feed
Cytisus x battandieri		Plant			
Cytisus praecox					
Digitalis				Sow	
Epilobium			Feed		
Epimedium	Mulch	Mulch	Cut down		
Eryngium		Feed			
Euphorbia characias		Plant			
Euphorbia niciciana		Deadhead	Mulch		
Euphorbia polychroma		Feed			
Euphorbia robbiae			Mulch	Mulch	
Forsythia		Mulch	Mulch	Prune	
Fritillaria					
Fuchsia			Plant	Mulch	
Galtonia		Plant	Feed		

JULY	AUGUST	SEPTEMBER	OCTOBER	NOVEMBER	
Cuttings			Plant		**Clematis alpina**
Cuttings					**Clematis macropetala**
Cuttings			Plant		**Clematis 'Perle d'Azur'**
					Clematis viticella
	Mulch	Plant	Plant	Divide	**Convallaria**
Cuttings	Cuttings		Plant	Divide	**Corylopsis**
		Layer	Plant		**Cotinus**
	*Prune			Plant	**Crataegus**
		Plant	Plant		**Crocus**
			Plant		**Crocus speciosus**
	Sow	Plant	Plant	Feed	**Cyclamen coum**
	Sow		Plant		**Cyclamen hederifolium**
Cuttings	*Prune				**Cytisus x battandieri**
*Prune		Cuttings	Plant		**Cytisus praecox**
			Plant		**Digitalis**
		Divide	Plant		**Epilobium**
			Plant		**Epimedium**
			Plant	Cut down	**Eryngium**
		Plant	Mulch		**Euphorbia characias**
		Cuttings	Plant		**Euphorbia niciciana**
			Divide	Cut down	**Euphorbia polychroma**
		Plant	Divide		**Euphorbia robbiae**
			Cuttings	Plant	**Forsythia**
		Plant	Plant		**Fritillaria**
			Cuttings	Protect	**Fuchsia**
					Galtonia

	FEBRUARY	MARCH	APRIL	MAY	JUNE
Geranium		Feed	Plant		
Gladiolus					Feed
Hedera	*Prune	*Prune	Mulch		
Helleborus argutifolius	Cut down	Mulch	Mulch		
Helleborus orientalis	Cut down	Mulch	Mulch		
Hemerocallis		Plant			
Humulus		Plant	Mulch		
Hydrangea		Plant	Mulch		
Iris			Feed		
Kirengeshoma		Sow	Plant	Mulch	
Leucojum					Divide
Ligustrum		Plant	Mulch	*Prune	
Lilium		Mulch	Plant		Feed
Liriope		Plant	Divide		
Lonicera		Mulch	Prune		
Lunaria				Sow	Sow
Macleaya		Mulch	Divide		
Magnolia stellata	Layer	Mulch	Plant		
Mahonia		Mulch	*Prune	Plant	
Malus	*Prune		Mulch		
Mentha		Plant			
Miscanthus		Cut down	Divide		
Narcissus			Deadhead	Deadhead	
Nepeta		Divide	Feed		
Nerine			Plant		
Nicotiana	Sow	Sow		Plant	

JULY	AUGUST	SEPTEMBER	OCTOBER	NOVEMBER	
			Divide	Cut down	**Geranium**
	Divide		Cut down	Plant	**Gladiolus**
Cuttings	Cuttings		Plant		**Hedera**
Sow			Plant		**Helleborus argutifolius**
Sow			Plant		**Helleborus orientalis**
		Cut down	Plant	Divide	**Hemerocallis**
			Prune		**Humulus**
	Cuttings		Plant	Deadhead	**Hydrangea**
		Plant	Divide		**Iris**
					Kirengeshoma
		Plant	Plant		**Leucojum**
		*Prune	Cuttings	Plant	**Ligustrum**
		Plant	Cut down	Protect	**Lilium**
					Liriope
*Prune	Cuttings		Plant	Plant	**Lonicera**
		Plant			**Lunaria**
			Plant	Cut down	**Macleaya**
					Magnolia stellata
Cuttings					**Mahonia**
			Plant		**Malus**
			Plant	Divide	**Mentha**
			Mulch		**Miscanthus**
Divide		Plant			**Narcissus**
				Cut down	**Nepeta**
			Protect		**Nerine**
					Nicotiana

	FEBRUARY	MARCH	APRIL	MAY	JUNE
Nigella		Sow			
Oenothera		Cut down	Divide		
Omphalodes		Sow	Plant		
Osmanthus			Mulch		
Parthenocissus		Plant			
Penstemon			Plant		Feed
Phalaris		Feed			
Philadelphus		Mulch			
Phlox		Plant	Feed		
Polemonium		Divide	Feed		
Prunus x cistena		Mulch	Mulch		*Prune
Pulmonaria		Mulch	Mulch		
Pyrus	Feed	Mulch			
Romneya		Feed	Plant	Divide	
Rose		Mulch			
Rubus			Mulch		Prune
Salvia		Sow		Plant	
Scilla					
Sedum		Plant	Divide	Mulch	Stake
Sternbergia					
Symphytum		Feed			
Tulip					Deadhead
Verbena		Sow		Plant	
Viburnum	Mulch				
Viola	Feed	Plant			
Yucca	Propagate	Plant			

JULY	AUGUST	SEPTEMBER	OCTOBER	NOVEMBER	
					Nigella
			Plant		**Oenothera**
Divide					**Omphalodes**
Cuttings			Plant		**Osmanthus**
Prune	Cuttings	Cuttings		Plant	**Parthenocissus**
		Cuttings	Cut down	Protect	**Penstemon**
			Plant	Cut down	**Phalaris**
			Plant		**Philadelphus**
			Cut down	Divide	**Phlox**
				Cut down	**Polemonium**
					Prunus x cistena
			Divide	Protect	**Pulmonaria**
			Plant	Prune	**Pyrus**
			Cut down		**Romneya**
			Cuttings	Plant	**Rose**
	Cuttings			Plant	**Rubus**
				Protect	**Salvia**
		Plant	Plant		**Scilla**
				Cut down	**Sedum**
	Plant	Plant			**Sternbergia**
		Plant	Divide	Cut down	**Symphytum**
				Plant	**Tulip**
				Protect	**Verbena**
				Plant	**Viburnum**
Sow	Trim		Plant		**Viola**
					Yucca

INDEX